WRITTEN JUST FOR YOU

What I really want you to know.

Roy W. Harris

In the book...................

CAREER

Keep Your Word

Strive For Excellence

FINANCES

10, 10, 80 – Handle Your Money Well

You Should Tithe

MORE THINGS TO REMEMBER

Final Thoughts from Pawpaw

Introduction

A word spoken at the right time is like gold apples on a silver tray. Proverbs 25:11*(ESV)*

I am truly a fortunate man. God blessed me with two *wonderful wives* Amy and Diana (who died from complications of breast cancer.) I married above myself both times.

He blessed me with two great children, Missy and Aaron who I'm very proud of and also proud of their spouses Tim and Susan. I've seen many grandchildren around the world and I know *beyond a doubt,* I have *the finest grandchildren* in the entire world.

What is the greatest gift one can give to his children and grandchildren? Is it money, gold, silver, houses, land or a large material inheritance? What legacy can one leave that will help them find the keys to happiness, success and contentment?

Conveying Biblical principles and lessons learned from decades of living is more valuable than material possessions. I believe the greatest legacy one can leave to others is these proven keys to happiness, success and contentment.

Written on the pages that follow is my gift to those I deeply love. Blood of my blood and bone of my bones, they are more precious to me than life itself.

My prayer is that they will think of me as a man who loved life and lived it to the fullest. They will think of my life as one that was well lived.

The book is filled with funny stories, serious stories, life lessons, Biblical truths, moral principles, practical suggestions, advice on personal life, family life, spiritual life, professional life and how to handle finances.

This book can be a great resource for others also. Parents, grandparents, youth group leaders, pastors, small groups may find this as a great resource to life lessons that can impact others in a positive way.

Special Recognition

Marissa

Marissa – You are *my favorite first grandchild*. Your smile and caring heart always warms up a room. You are special *period*, but especially because you made me a Pawpaw. I know God has great things in store for you. Always know I will be on the sidelines *cheering you on* in the game of life. I am anxious to see where God leads you what He does with your life. Pawpaw loves you.

Mason

Mason – You are *my favorite grandson*. You are one of the finest young men I know. Your attitude of preferring others before yourself and choosing to treat others with kindness and generosity will take you far in life. Always know how proud I am of you and how much I brag on you to others. I am excited to see the future and what God will do with your life. Pawpaw loves you.

Claire

Claire – You are *my favorite middle grandchild*. This photo is such a clear picture of who you are. You are looking out over the ocean with awe and wonder. You have a great sense of humor with an ability to put your thoughts and feelings into words on paper. Keep reading and keep writing! You will impact many people and you will change the world. Pawpaw loves you.

Lauren

Lauren – You are *my favorite next to the youngest grandchild*. Your quiet ways and hard work ethic inspires me. Your love for animals shows your compassionate side. Yet you compete in sports with a drive to do your best that will carry you far in life. You are my athlete. Running cross-country and playing basketball are two sports we have in common. Your hard work ethic makes me proud. You will stand tall and rise above your peers as you continue to never quit or give up. Always know that I am very proud of you. Pawpaw loves you.

Rachel

Rachel – You are *my favorite youngest grandchild*. This photo captures your personality in a nutshell. You are one of the most outgoing little girls I know. You always have a smile on your face and your *have fun personality* makes everyone around you feel good. You are also special because you are my youngest grandchild. You bring me a great deal of joy and happiness. I am looking forward to watching you grow and see what God will do with your wonderful outgoing personality. Pawpaw loves you.

Personal Life

Don't Run From Your Problems

When one mentions home, a stream of emotions and memories flood the mind. It would be impossible to summarize eighteen years of *home living* in one short story. But one might remember an event or two that proved to be truly life changing. One such event comes to mind for this writer.

I'm not sure how old I was but I must have been around eight or nine. I'd spent most of my young life living on a dead end street and East 16th Street was a great place to live.

The little white two-bedroom house at the end of the street was strategically located. It was bordered on three sides with opportunities for make believe, exploration and adventure.

The great White River flowed a few hundred yards behind the house. It required adult supervision for its periodic visits, but was a great place of adventure nonetheless. Woodlands complete with a small trickling brook flanked our bedroom side of the house. It provided opportunities for me to be *all boy*.

Across the street was a huge field. A single line of trees separated the field from the little white house. The limbs on the trees hung perfectly enabling me to climb them like the monkey bars at a children's playground.

The field was full of places to explore and things to do. It provided a place for March winds to lift paper kites with torn homemade rag tails and a hundred feet of white twine to heights only dreamed of the night before.

In the middle of the field was a dug out area that was perfect for playing army with toy guns, tanks and soldiers. The field offered me a measure of independence and freedom. This was one of the few places on earth I could travel beyond the boundaries of my 16th Street yard.

Oh yes, there were others who enjoyed the field and made it special. The Simmons boys lived two houses away and there were several children in that family. Most were older but two were close to my age. Unfortunately, their influence was not always the best.

I was playing in the field one afternoon when Marcus (AKA Bug) came running across the street and into the field. His father was hot on his heels. His father was out of breath and stopped at the edge of the field.

Marcus' father gazed at the fading image of Marcus for a few minutes, then turned, walked back across the street and back into his house. Marcus said that this happened all the time. He'd get in trouble and run for it. His dad was a heavy drinker and would eventually give up and forget about him so Marcus would be off the hook.

I filed this away in the back of my mind for future use. Then one day it happened. I got in trouble with Dad. On an impulse, while remembering the success of my friend Marcus, I thought it might be worth a try.

Oh... That was not the best decision I'd ever made in my young life. I ran toward the field at a hard gallop, knowing my father would probably chase and catch me. I gave a quick glance over my shoulder as I cleared the tree line.

Dad had not moved. Not a single step forward or backward, just a stern stare in my direction. "Wow, maybe this is going to work," I thought. I did not realize that time was on my dad's side.

I ran for the safety of the dugout bunker. After taking up a defensive position, expecting my father to overrun the bunker at any moment and rain down *a belt of destruction* on me, I was pleasantly surprised to see an empty field with no one in sight.

Minutes seemed like hours, yet nothing was happening. I sat in the dirt all alone. I didn't know what to do. I'd temporarily escaped my father's impending wrath – but now what?

I realized that I couldn't stay in the field forever. It might be wise to scout the perimeter and see where Dad was. I worked my way to the far end of the field thinking it would be better to approach the house from another angle, hopefully undetected by Dad.

I entered the tree line and moved slowly along the edge of the trees until I gained a clear view of our yard and house. What was this? Dad had walked back to the front porch and was seated comfortably on the steps. This totally confused me. Why would he do that? Why hadn't he come looking for me? Was he still upset? Maybe this was going to work after all!

Not sure of what was happening, I retreated back into the woods, hoping I was out of my father's sight, to think more about this. Maybe I should take a second look. I moved cautiously back to my vantage point hoping my father had gone inside the house.

Oh, no! He hadn't moved. He even seemed relaxed and as though he might sit there all day. An uneasy feeling began to creep into my mind and drifted slowly down to the pit of my stomach. Maybe Dad was not going to leave the porch at all. Maybe he was simply waiting for me to come home.

I retreated back into the woods one final time. I was getting hungry. It was almost suppertime. The thought began to cross my mind, *I want to go home*. I was all alone. No security of my father's approval and protection. No enjoyment of my mother's comfort and provisions. I was in the cold damp woods with no hope of things getting better unless I went home.

One final time, I entered the field from the far end of the woods. It seemed like I'd walked a hundred miles. I could see the house in the distance. Dad was still sitting on the steps looking in my direction.

Step after step, I drew closer and closer to the edge of the field and home. Dad didn't move. Dad rose to his feet as I crossed the street and stepped into the front yard.

I wish I could say he swept me up into arms and told me everything was forgiven and there'd be no punishment, but a lesson needed to be learned from this experience. I received two spankings that day. The first one was for what I'd done wrong to begin with (I still don't remember what it was even to this day). The second one was for running away (I'll never forget that one).

I was welcomed back into the house after the punishment

had been administered. I took my usual place at the table and once again began enjoying the benefits of being part of the Harris family.

I remember asking my dad many years later why he just sat on the porch and didn't come after me. He answered, "You were never out of my sight, and I knew you had nowhere else to go and would eventually come home."

Always Remember

I learned some great lessons that day that have served me well in life.

- One lesson is that you cannot run away from your problems. In the end it will cost you more. You are better off to deal with difficult issues earlier rather than later.
- A second lesson is there is no place like home. The world is cold and uncaring. Whether you are a child or an adult home is the place you want to be.
- For those of us who know the Lord and His Word, I believe there is a possible spiritual application to this story as well. God is one who loves us dearly. He loves us enough to allow us to choose how we will live.
- When we make mistakes, do wrong and wander away from Him, He still loves us and seeks to guide us back to Him. Although we may be out of His will, we are never out of His sight.
- He understands and waits for us to remember that we have no place else to go. He waits for us to miss the protection of

His strong arms, the comfort of His satisfying provisions and the warmth of being part of His secure household. He never runs away from us, we run away from Him.

- Turning away from our wrongdoing and sin is not easy. When we make that first step towards home, God leaves the porch and races across the yard to meet us. Sometimes we must endure the consequences because of our mistakes, but in the end, our place at His table has been reserved. We remain part of His divine household and we'll spend all eternity under His protection and care.

- In order to enjoy God's blessings, one must first develop a personal relationship with Him. This begins by realizing that something is missing in one's life. That something is someone and that someone is Jesus Christ. If you admit to God you are a sinner, believe that Christ died on the cross for your sins and can save you and, by faith, ask Him to, He promises in His Word that He will come into your heart and change your life. If you haven't done that, let me encourage you to do that today.

- There are times when we all wish we could be like Dorothy in *The Wizard of Oz* and click our heels three times and get back home. I will never forget when I ran away from home and came back the same day. One thing most of us believe: there is no place like home. One thing every Christian knows: there is no feeling like **coming home** and you can't run from your problems. They'll always come full circle and be waiting on you.

Never say Never

I had completed my service in the United States Army and returned to finish my bachelor's degree at Free Will Baptist Bible College (now Welch College) in Nashville, Tennessee.

We were living in a basement apartment on Murphy Road in the Sylvan Park area near the 3606 West End Avenue campus. The year was 1975 or 76. I was about 22 or 23 years old. Our daughter Missy was two years old and Aaron hadn't been born yet.

I earned a bit of a reputation helping friends diagnose and repair car mechanical problems and installing new sound systems. I was installing a new sound system in one of my friend's cars when I encountered a small problem and knew it could be one of two things.

I drove to Kmart, a huge department store on Charlotte Avenue, a few miles from our apartment. Kmart was the first big department store chain, before Walmart became available in most cities across America.

I purchased the two parts I needed and headed back home. I used one of the parts to fix the problem and a few days later returned the other one that I didn't need back to Kmart to get a refund.

The customer service lady at Kmart informed me that the store did not give refunds on electrical parts. I was furious! My young temper got the best of me and I began arguing with the lady.

I explained that I hadn't used the part and it was still brand new. She was not very understanding and a bit rude. The more we talked the more upset I became. I finally had enough! I blurted out, "Ok, if that's the way you feel about it, I'll never set foot in this store again." I left the part on the counter and walked out of the store.

I'd shown her, I thought. I began to cool off and the closer I got to our apartment, the more I felt a sinking feeling in the pit of my stomach.

I began to realize something and realized it even more in the coming months. I had walked out of the best place to find about anything we needed to buy as a family. Kmart also had the best prices in town.

I made the statement that I'd never set foot in that store again. Now I had to live with that. I could never go to that Kmart store again in order to keep my word.

We had to shop in other smaller stores and sometimes drive much further to buy the things we needed. I learned some valuable lessons from that experience.

Always Remember

- Choose your words carefully. Before you speak, take a moment and step back, take a breath and think about what you are about to say. This may keep you from saying something you might regret later.

- Be careful about using the word *never.* I said I would *never* set foot back in that Kmart store. What a huge mistake I made! I cut off one of my favorite, best priced, and most convenient places to shop.

- Using the word *never* may cause you to tell a lie. Saying things like: I'll never speak to you again, I'll never go there again, I'll never watch that again, I'll never eat that again, I'll never wear that again, etc. may be hard words to swallow.

Be Honest

Never take anything that doesn't belong to you. Always be the kind of person who is honest, even when no one sees what you are doing.

Pay Less Supermarket, located across the street from Southside Junior High School, was a popular meeting place. Sparky and my other friends would often meet outside the market in the mornings before school began. We would occasionally drift inside the store on cold days to warm up from the cold Indiana winter weather. This story is about one of those winter mornings.

My parents made sure I had all the things I needed - food, shelter, clothing and also notebooks, paper, pens, pencils, etc. I always had lunch money and if my needs required more for special class projects or outings, the money was there.

It was cold outside that day and Sparky invited me to join him for a stroll inside the market. Sparky told me that he was going to *cop some notebook paper*. He told me that he'd taken several items from the store before. We entered the store and Sparky headed straight for the school supplies aisle.

I watched as Sparky stopped in front of the shelves containing the packages of neatly stacked white notebook paper. I could hardly believe what I was seeing. Sparky looked one way then the other, reached up, grabbed a plastic wrapped 250 count package of paper and slipped it into his notebook. He looked over at me and said, "You take something too."

I had my eye on a twelve-inch *Red Ruler* for several days. I hadn't mentioned it to my parents, probably because at age twelve, my mind refocused often and I didn't give much thought to the *Red Ruler* unless I was in the store.

I hesitated for a second, but with Sparky's encouragement, I grabbed the ruler. What should I do with it now? I quickly slid the ruler over the inside of my left wrist and up my coat sleeve. There, I'd done it. I had the ruler, now what would I do?

A troubling feeling began to sweep over me. I'd grown up around men and women of character who taught me not to take things that didn't belong to me. I knew the Ten Commandments. I wasn't sure which number it was, but I was absolutely certain that one of them said: *Thou shalt not steal*. Yes, *steal!* I was about to *steal* the *Red Ruler*.

The words seemed to replay like a Power Point Presentation over and over in my mind. I was stealing! I was about to become a thief.

Sparky said, "Let's buy a candy bar." I had an idea the reason for purchasing the candy was a diversion so no one would suspect what we were really doing.

The *Red Ruler* was out of sight, but somehow not out of mind. It was no longer as appealing as it had been before. It was up my sleeve, but what could I do? It was like holding a mean dog by the ears. You know you need to let go, but you dare not because you're afraid what the dog might do if you turn him loose. Somehow I knew that I should not go out the exit door with that ruler.

But how could I put it back? What if someone saw me pull it from my sleeve? What would Sparky say to the other fellows outside of the store if I didn't go through with it?

We made our way through the checkout line. With each step forward, I felt my heart pounding harder and louder. Surely the man in front of me heard it.

With candy bar in hand, I watched as Sparky paid. I just couldn't go through with it. I quietly slid the *Red Ruler* from my coat sleeve and laid it on the candy bar rack hoping no one had seen any of this whole mess.

My emotions were hard to describe. I felt a sense of *relief* because I hadn't done something that deep down inside I knew was wrong. I felt a sense of *shame*. How could I have even thought of doing something like this? I felt a sense of *disgust*. Why had I let someone talk me into something that might have gotten me into a lot of trouble?

Glad to have this whole ordeal about over, I made my way to the store exit. Sparky was walking a few steps ahead of you. The automatic doors swung outward and we walked out of the store.

Before the doors could close behind us, someone came running through them behind us. I watched helplessly as the store manager grabbed Sparky by the arm and demanded he open his notebook.

Sparky's face changed from a healthy pink shade to a blood drained white as he opened his notebook and the stolen paper fell out. The manager grabbed him by the back of the neck with one hand and held the stolen paper in the other. He marched poor Sparky back through the automatic entry doors.

The manager halfway turned toward me and said something I have never forgotten, "Aren't you glad you put the ruler back?" The manager had seen the whole thing. Even though I didn't answer out loud, I sure was glad I'd put the *Red Ruler* back.

As Sparky and the manager disappeared inside the store to regions unknown, I walked slowly towards the school crossing. I wasn't sure of all that had just taken place but I was stunned and almost numb, yet so thankful I hadn't taken that *Red Ruler*.

Sparky never made it to class that day. He returned a day or two later and briefed me about what had taken place in the store. Sparky had been taken to the manager's office where he was soon joined by a couple of Anderson's finest (two police officers). His parents were called and Sparky was in a heap a trouble.

Always Remember

I learned some important lessons from the *Red Ruler* chapter of my life.

- *First* of all, I learned that a person should be careful not to hang around the wrong kind of friends. People who want you to do things that you know deep down inside are wrong are not really your friends. They care little about you or what kind of trouble they may cause you.

- A *second lesson* learned was that when you take something that isn't yours and didn't pay for, it is stealing. Stealing is breaking one of God's commandments and is *wrong*. It is a sin against God. My advice to you is never, never, never take anything that doesn't belong to you. The *guilt* and *shame* one experiences are not worth it.

- A *third lesson* learned was to *listen* to that small voice that speaks to you from deep down inside. Adults call this a conscience. When it tells you, *don't do that,* listen and do what it says – *just don't do that*.

Eventually I got my *Red Ruler*, No, not that year or the next. I grew up and became a pastor. I preached a sermon one Sunday morning many years later and told this story to my congregation to illustrate a needed lesson. One of my church members named Larry Powell surprised me a few days later with a nice bright *Red Ruler*. I keep it on my desk today.

It always pays to be honest. Be an honest person; you'll be glad you did.

You aren't entitled to anything.

My father Albert Harris was born on May 3, 1931, and was the youngest of four children. He grew up on a small farm in the Thorn Gap Community near Monterey, Tennessee.

His parents worked hard at eking out a living providing food, shelter and clothing for their family. They raised their own vegetables for food and sold strawberries and tobacco as cash crops, which provided money to purchase the other things they needed.

The children were expected to do their share of the work and most would quit school after the eighth grade. Dad and Mom, Fannie Mae (Brown) Harris, were married on April 7, 1951. I remember Dad telling me that he realized early that he didn't see much of a future in trying to make a living in the area where he grew up.

He learned of the possibility of a better life with good paying automobile industry jobs in Anderson, Indiana. He'd never travelled more than a few miles away from home but made the decision to see what might lie over the horizon.

He *hired in,* as he likes to describe it at Delco Remy and would remain with the company for the next 34 years. Dad was a great worker and missed only a handful of days of work during those three and a half decades.

My brother Rick and I enjoyed a great life. Dad and Mom both worked outside the home, but we lived the American Dream with them. We began our journey living in a small two-bedroom home at the end of East 16th Street in Anderson. Mom and Dad worked hard and managed their money well. We moved to 3709 East Lynn Street in a better area of town when I was eleven years old.

They were able to build a new brick home on West 25th Street near our church in one of the best school districts in Anderson when I began my sophomore year of high school.

Dad and Mom came from backgrounds where they had very little growing up. They knew their parents couldn't help them so if they were to be successful, they would have to work hard and do it on their own.

They were *very successful*. They've been retired for many years. They are both in their mid-eighties and still get up early every morning and find something productive and worthwhile to do.

They worked hard to make sure we had food, shelter and clothing and all the basic things we needed. They made sure that Christmas was special every year and we had many things that we wanted.

Dad made arrangements a few months before he retired to take me on a personal tour of a few of the Delco Remy factories in Anderson where he'd worked. I was amazed at some of the hard jobs he'd labored at and the kind of work he'd done.

One job stands out in my mind. We walked through the exterior doors to what was called *The Foundry*. The inside temperature was over 100 degrees and I could immediately feel a blast of hot air on my skin. Casings for automobile starters and generators were made in *The Foundry.*

Metal was heated until it became soft in a liquid form, then it was poured into molds that formed starter and generator casings. Some of the men knew Dad and spoke to him while the shift foreman walked me through the process from beginning to end.

We walked off the shop floor into a break/rest area. I remember asking Dad how could he stand working in such a hot place. "We'd work about 20 minutes and then step in here for 10. Then back for another 20 minutes. We'd take a 30-minute lunch break and repeat the process all day long."

Always Remember

I have tremendous respect for my father. I gained even more respect after seeing the jobs he'd done and how hard he worked to provide for his family. He and Mom instilled in Rick and me a number of things that have guided our lives and helped us become successful in our personal lives, our families and our spiritual lives.

- No one owes you anything. We shouldn't live our lives thinking that our parents, society, the government, our bosses or neighbors owe us something. They do not!
- You are not entitled to anything. The world really doesn't care about your last name or how important you may think you are.
- Just because you are the child of your parents doesn't mean your parents should be responsible for your every wish and desire.
- If you want some new electronic gadget, a car, your own

place, work for it.

- Your parents are not responsible for taking care of you the rest of your life. You must take responsibility and provide for your own needs. Just as your mom and dad made lives for themselves, you need to be working towards the same.

It's never right to do the wrong thing.

It was September 1966 and I was about to begin my freshman year at Southside Junior High School. My basketball coach, Mr. Delph, required the ballplayers to run on the cross-country team in the fall to be in good physical condition when the basketball season started a couple of months later.

The cross-country coach had also been my seventh grade basketball coach. The first day was not an *official* day at school, but we were to come by for a short period of time and pick up a list of what books and supplies we'd need for the coming year.

My uncle Earnest had married Hazel a short time before and was moving into a new apartment on this same day. He asked me the day before if I'd help him move. I agreed to help and rode my bicycle to school that day.

I was supposed to stay for cross-country practice after school, but hopped on my bike and rode to my Uncle's place with my cross-country sweats and running shoes in tow.

I helped him move during the afternoon and eventually rode home. I was surprised to see my mother's car in our driveway and knew something could be wrong. She was home early! I'd planned to arrive before she or Dad did and conceal the fact that I'd skipped practice.

I rode into the garage behind our house on East Lynn Street and parked my bicycle. I walked up the steps, opened the door, and walked through the kitchen, through the hallway and into our den.

Mom was sitting on the couch to my left. She turned facing

me and said, "Where have you been?"

I said, "Wow I'm tired. I just finished cross-country practice."

"You did no such thing," she said emphatically. The blood drained from my face and my heart began to pound as though it was coming out of my chest. "I just came from South Side and your coach said he hadn't seen you."

Then I remembered! Mom was going to take off work early and come by to help me purchase my books and supplies at school before practice. She began to review the time she'd spent in the parking lot waiting in the car to meet me. After an hour had passed, she saw the cross-country team practicing behind the school and walked over thinking that I'd forgotten, but I wasn't there.

She was not happy! So she asked me again, "Where have you been and don't lie to me this time?"

I explained that this was a noble thing I'd done in helping Uncle Ernest move. I tried to rationalize that even though I'd done something wrong, it was for a good reason.

She was not impressed or convinced. "Just wait until your dad gets home," she said. Those were the kind of words that cause *fear* and *trembling* in the heart of a 14-year-old high school freshman. I must admit I was scared because my father had instilled in me a reverential respect and when I knew I would have to answer to him, it elevated the seriousness of the situation to a much higher level.

Mom didn't say a word to me until Dad arrived home later that evening. I sat in the den fearing the future and trying to rehearse some words that might somehow get me out of this mess. The words didn't come easily.

The old 1954 Ford pickup truck rattled into our driveway and came to a stop. The engine stopped and I heard the truck door close. This was it! Mom met Dad at the back door. "We've got a problem with your son," she said.

"What's the problem?" Dad asked.

They walked into the den and Mom began to review the events of the past few hours. The frown on Dad's face changed to upset and I knew I was in big trouble.

"I ought to wear you out," (give you a spanking with a belt) he said. I felt a small glimmer of hope that I might get out of this somehow. Mom was having none of it. My flicker of hope was quickly snuffed out with Mom's words, "If you don't spank him, I'll never tell you anything else."

Oh my, all hope was lost. He pulled off his belt and *wore me out* right then and there. He also told me that I was not to go to my uncle's house for any reason unless I got permission from him or Mom.

Mom didn't stop there. She called her brother, my uncle, and gave him a piece of her mind and let him know she held him responsible.

Always Remember

We eventually were able to patch things up with the whole family and my uncle even stayed in my home on a few occasions after I had grown up and married. My Uncle Ernest passed away years ago.

I learned some valuable lessons from that experience.

- It is *never right* to do the *wrong thing*. There is something called situational ethics. A simple definition is that people sometimes decide on what they think is the right thing to do based on the situation they find themselves in.

- Do not wait until you find yourself in a difficult situation to decide what is right or wrong. You might make the wrong decision because, like I did with my uncle, you make yourself believe that because you want to do a good thing, it is okay to do something wrong in order to accomplish it.

- We should develop our belief in what is right and wrong before we find ourselves in difficult situations.

- We must have something to guide us. The Bible, God's Word is the best source. We should decide what is right or wrong based on the Bible. What are some of those things?
  - It is always wrong to lie.
  - It is always wrong to take anything that doesn't belong to us without permission.
  - It is always wrong to talk back to our parents.
  - It is always wrong to cheat.
  - It is always wrong to make fun of others.

- It is never right to do something wrong. Even if the thing you want to do is good, it is not right if you have to do something wrong to accomplish it. Make up your mind that you are going to always do the right thing. If you do that, then you will not allow yourself to do something wrong and justify it by saying it was for the right reason. It is still wrong!

Always do the right thing

We were living in Savannah, Georgia in the early 1990s and I had the honor of pastoring the Savannah First Free Will Baptist Church.

I remember receiving a check but I cannot remember who it was from or for how much. I endorsed it and stopped by the bank to cash it. I made my way through the bank's drive-thru and placed the check along with my driver's license in the drawer and in a few moments had my cash.

I drove around the bank and started to pull back onto Derenne Avenue when I realized the bank teller had given me too much money.

I immediately got back in line and made my way to the drive-thru window. The lady asked, "How can I help you?" I responded by telling her that she'd given me 11 cents too much. She opened the drawer and I placed the 11 cents back in. The 11 cents wasn't mine and the right thing to do was give it back. She thanked me and I didn't think any more about it.

A few days passed and I stopped by the bank to take care of some business. I went inside the bank this time. I stepped up to the counter and handed one of the ladies my deposit. She read my name and did something that took me totally by surprise. She said, "You're the man who returned the 11 cents the other day, aren't you?" I was almost embarrassed but agreed that I was.

Then she announced to the whole bank, "This is Roy Harris, the man who returned the 11 cents the other day." She thanked me again for my honesty and for doing the right thing. She explained she was working the drive-thru that day when I came through and returned the money. She told the entire staff in a meeting earlier about the 11 cents and my returning it.

I was not looking for accolades or recognition. I returned the money because it was right to do the right thing.

Always Remember

- Always do the right thing! Sometimes doing the right thing will be easy. Sometimes doing the right thing will be hard.
- Remember – someone may be watching you. Don't do the right thing to impress anyone, but you should be aware that others see how you live and what you do (and don't do).
- Do the right thing even if you think no one is watching.
- Remember that God is always watching. The real you is who you are when you think no one is around. Always remember that God is omnipresent (He's everywhere all the time). God is everywhere you are all the time. God knows when you do the right thing. God also knows when you do not do the right thing.
- There is a good feeling that comes from doing the right thing: self-respect, a clear conscience and a sense of knowing YOU did the right thing.
- There is a sinking feeling that comes from not doing the right thing: loss of self-respect, a guilty conscience, a sense of knowing YOU didn't do what you knew you should have done.

Doing the *right thing* is *always* the *right thing* to do.

        So

            always

                do

                  the

                     right

                        thing!

You'll be glad you did!

Be Kind to Others

Kindness is a free gift that can be shared with everyone. It costs you nothing, but its value is above anything money can buy.

I remember receiving a phone call on a Sunday afternoon in 1991. The gentleman on the other end introduced himself as Bill Arbon, chairman of the Board of Deacons at the First Free Will Baptist Church in Savannah, Georgia. I was presently serving as the Dean of Students at what is now Welch College and felt God's direction in leaving the college and returning to the pastorate.

I immediately found a kinship with Brother Bill. I was impressed with his demeanor over the phone and the kind way he treated me. He called representing the church to ask if I would consider pastoring the Savannah church. After praying and seeking God's direction, I eventually accepted their offer to become their pastor.

Bill was the greeter who welcomed people to the services at the front door of our church. His winning smile and kind voice gave the best first impression a church could give.

My daughter Missy was a student of Welch College in Nashville, TN and my son Aaron was in high school at Jenkins High in Savannah.

Money was tight but we desperately needed a second vehicle. One of my former students, Bennie, originally from our church in Savannah, worked for a man who owned a car rental company in Nashville who also had been one of my students. The company often sold their rental cars when they reached a certain mileage level.

Bennie came home to Savannah for a visit and we talked a little before church and I asked him how he and his family were doing. During our conversation, my need for a second car came up. He mentioned that the company was about to sell a couple of Chevrolet Geo Metros and wanted to know if I might be interested in one of them? He told me that because of my relationship with him and the owner of the company who was also one of my former students, he might be able to get me one of the cars for $1,300, a very generous offer. I told Bennie that I'd get back to him in a week or so.

When I arrived at church on Wednesday night, Bill Arbon asked me if he could speak privately with me. Well, anytime the chairman of the deacon board wants to talk with you privately you feel a small twinge of anxiety. We stepped into the church Sunday school office and closed the door. Bill asked, "When can we go to Nashville and pick up that car?"

I responded, "The car is just what we need but we can't afford it right now."

"I believe there is a way you can," he said while reaching for something in his pocket. Bill pulled out 13 one hundred dollar bills and offered to give me the money to pay for the car. I thanked him, but insisted that we consider this a loan and we agree on a plan for repayment. He reluctantly consented but insisted that no interest would be paid. I asked if $100 a month for 13 months would work for him. He said that would be fine but if I needed to miss a month now and then, that would be absolutely fine.

I paid him $100 per month for 10 months ($1,000 of the $1,300). When I attempted to make the 11th payment, he refused to take the money and said, "Pastor, your account is paid in full. I love and appreciate you and your love for our church; this is the least I can do."

Bill Arbon is in heaven now, but I'll never forget him. He was one of the kindest men I've ever known.

Always Remember

- It is never "ok" to be unkind to anyone for any reason. Even when people are not kind to us, we should be kind to them.
- Who should you be kind to? Everyone!
- Look for ways to show kindness.
- Open doors for people who have their hands full.
- When your used paper towel misses the trash can in the restroom, pick it up and place it in the trash can. Someone will have to do the dirty job of cleaning that restroom so pick up the paper towel you left on the floor.
- Speak kindly to people you come in contact with. Don't be rude, ignore or talk ugly to them.
- Be courteous to servers in restaurants. They're on their feet for many hours and work very hard and make very little money.
- Never make fun of or talk down to people who are less fortunate than you.
- Never make fun of other people's looks. We tend to look at the outside but God looks at the person's heart. (1 Samuel 16:7)

Take Responsibility for Your Actions

I was awakened by the smell of homemade biscuits rising softly from the oak fired cook stove and quietly hanging like an invisible cloud over the bed. The sun still had a good hour to travel before rising in the morning sky.

Mammy (my grandmother) had been busy in the kitchen since 4:00 am preparing biscuits from scratch along with fried chicken (yes, fried chicken for breakfast) and her family trophy winning chocolate gravy. We dressed quickly and made our way through the early dawn to the barn 100 yards or so away. The biting cold morning air was forgotten as we placed the bucket in the proper place and old Betsy yielded her cream rich milk.

We soon found ourselves back at the house and seated on long benches beside the large table surrounded by a morning feast fit for Harris & Brown royalty. Biscuits, fried chicken and oh yes, that wonderful chocolate gravy. After breakfast, Mom, Dad, my brother and I piled into the car and headed a few miles into the hills to the Thorn Gap community where my Grandma and Grandpa Harris lived.

Billy Lee Livingston was a legend in our minds. He was bigger than life with his stretch suspenders and long sleeve shirt moving from the gas pumps, to slicing bologna, to punching keys on the manual cash register.

The car lumbered down the big hill and coasted into the small parking lot beside Billy Lee's Store. I couldn't wait to get inside. I knew there would be a cold Dr. Pepper waiting for me. But more importantly, Dad had given me 50 cents to buy a box of 22 rifle shells.

I knew exactly where the gun ammunition was in Billy Lee's store. I breezed through the door and around the black pot belly stove making a beeline for the shells. I quickly picked up a box and plunked them and my 50 cents down on the counter. I'd completely forgotten about my Dr. Pepper.

Uncle Luke, my dad's older brother, lived up the hill behind Billy Lee's Store. We turned off the main road and into his driveway parking in front of his log farmhouse. Chickens were eagerly policing the front yard while two blue tick coonhounds barely lifted their heads when we set foot on the front porch.

The screen door opened and "Well looky who's here, come on in," the warm familiar voice of my aunt Betty ushered us into the living room in front of the blazing fireplace. My eyes automatically shifted to the right.

Lying neatly in a homemade gun rack above the bed was my uncle's 22 Winchester pump rifle. We visited a while then it was time to head to Grandma's house. My mind was on that rifle. I missed most of the conversation around me and was afraid that Dad was going to forget to ask my uncle if I could borrow his rifle.

I had borrowed it before and I was at the age when boys are working their way into becoming men and shooting guns was a rite of passage. As we stood preparing to leave, my glance dropped to the floor and then the words came, "Luke, Roy would like to borrow your rifle again if it's ok."

"Sure, he can," my uncle said walking towards the bed. He lifted the rifle from the rack and handed it to me. I can't describe the feeling of being 13 years old and walking to the car with a 22 rifle in my hands.

Our car rolled along the dirt road, rounded a curve and came to a stop in the driveway just beyond my grandparents' tin roofed two-bedroom house. A plume of grey white smoke rose lazily atop the hand-built rock fireplace and the smell of coal burning filled the air.

My grandfather with his long sleeved flannel shirt and familiar strapped blue bib overalls met us on the porch. Oh… it was so great to see him. Grandma was right behind him. You could feel the warm air rush through the open doorway, but there was something much warmer than the air. It was the unconditional love I felt each time I went to my grandparents' house. Hellos were said as we gathered around the pot belly stove and enjoyed just being together.

I left the rifle on the front porch leaning against the wall of the house. It was great to see my grandparents but my mind was on the adventure that waited on the porch. Finally, Dad asked Grandma if she had a couple of paper plates that I might use for targets. Since this was not the first time I'd brought the rifle to her house, she knew exactly what I needed. It seems like grandmothers have a knack for knowing just what it takes to please grandchildren.

Dad drew a big X on a plate and we tacked it to a tobacco stick, then walked across the dirt road and hammered the stick into the ground in front of the dirt bank. We walked back across the road and Dad said, "Son, it's all yours" and went back inside.

This was what I'd been looking forward to for weeks. I carefully pulled the box of 22 rifle shells out of my coat pocket, picked up the rifle and sat down in a wicker chair facing the road. I opened the latch that released the long loading tube so I could load the ammunition. I dropped one shell at a time into the rifle until it was completely loaded.

Now I must say, when it comes to weapons, I was a pretty good shot, especially for a 13 year old. I hit the target with every shot. I repeated the process of loading and firing one more time. I had fired 36 shells and had 14 left in my box of 50. I released the aluminum tube and slid it up making way for the shells to drop into the rifle as I had done the previous two times. I set the rifle down and leaned it against a porch post.

I bent down to pick up the box with the remaining shells. I'm not sure exactly what happened, but somehow my knee bumped the rifle, it fell off the porch and the aluminum tube hit the ground first. A feeling of panic swept over me. Maybe the fall from the porch didn't hurt the rifle. I leaped off the porch and grabbed the rifle. Oh no! The tube was bent. Maybe I could bend it back straight and everything would be all right.

I climbed the steps and sat back down in my chair gripping the rifle between my knees. I held the barrel of the gun with my left hand and began to bend the tube. It was easy to bend but I did not realize that once aluminum is bent, it cannot be bent back straight. I tried and tried for what seemed like an hour, but the tube just couldn't bend enough to slide back into the rifle.

Now what could I do? I was so afraid. How could I tell Dad? What would Uncle Luke think of me? I'd probably never get to use his rifle again. I might never get to use any rifle again.

It was cold outside and I was getting colder by the minute. It dawned on me that I couldn't stay on that porch for the rest of my life. I leaned the broken rifle back against the wall of the house and went inside.

I was quiet, much quieter than normal. I couldn't look at my dad for fear that he would see the despair in my eyes and ask me what was wrong. All of that was to no avail. Then the words came, "Where's the rifle?"

"It's on the porch," I said in a sheepish way.

"It got kind of quiet out there. What happened?" he asked.

How did he know that something happened? I told him that I had accidently knocked the rifle off the porch and bent the loading tube. We walked out on the porch together and he picked up the rifle.

I thought maybe Dad could fix it. He looked at it for a few minutes and said he couldn't. I told him how sorry I was and without hesitating he said, "I know you are son, but you'll have to tell your Uncle Luke what you did."

Oh no! I thought Dad would do that. We wouldn't see my uncle for at least a day or two. I wasn't sure if I should feel glad or sad about that. I thought about facing my Uncle Luke the rest of that day, that night and again the next day.

The day came and I would have to face what I had done. Even though it was an accident, I dreaded facing my uncle. I could feel a lump beginning to swell in my throat as we left the highway and turned into my uncle's driveway.

The car rolled to a stop and Dad and I got out. He carried the rifle and I followed him down the slate sidewalk onto the wood planked porch. The door opened and my uncle invited us in. It was very awkward. The three of us stood in my uncle's living room and my uncle sensed that something was wrong.

Dad spoke up, "Roy has something to tell you," handing him the rifle. I had rehearsed what I would say for two days but now the words did not come easily. I could hardly speak. I tried to explain what had happened and how sorry I was, but when I got to the being sorry part my quivering voice finally gave way to tears.

I was heartbroken because I felt that I had let my uncle down, disappointed my dad and failed in my struggle to become a man. Just as I thought my world was coming to an end, my uncle did the strangest thing.

He tossed the rifle on the bed as though it was not all that important. He dropped down on one knee, put his arm around me and somehow I knew it was going to be ok. He said, "Roy, don't you worry about that rifle. I have a good friend who is a gunsmith and I know for a fact that he has a spare loading tube in his shop. I'll run by there and pick one up and I'll have that rifle ready for you the next time you want it."

I could hardly believe what I was hearing. My tears dried up and my ruined world changed to one of joy. It all turned on a few words of understanding and forgiveness. My uncle did purchase a new loading tube and he had the 22 rifle waiting for me the next time we came to TN.

I honestly don't remember what I received for Christmas that year, but I can tell you what I received the next Christmas. A long narrow box appeared underneath the Christmas tree. Its dimensions were clearly consistent with the length and width of a 22 rifle.

You guessed it. I peeled off the wrapping paper, opened the box and a bolt action, magazine fed 22 caliber rifle with a fancy leather shoulder sling lay waiting for the hands of its new owner, me. All had been forgiven, though not forgotten by me, and my confidence had been restored. I had moved one step closer to manhood with this very important rite of passage. I now had my own 22 rifle.

Always Remember

I'm many years removed from that 13 year old's experience, but I have reflected many times and drawn from the lessons I learned from that very difficult experience.

- I learned that we all have accidents and make mistakes.

Some cannot be avoided and some can.

- I also realized when we make mistakes we have to face them and the sooner the better. They won't just go away.
- We usually save ourselves a lot of worry and trouble by owning up to what we've done as soon as possible.
- I learned that those who truly love us do so even when we make mistakes.
- I learned that mistakes are generally short-term events and that life will get better.

When you make mistakes, and you will, always take responsibility for your actions. You'll be glad you did when it's all over.

Forgive and Try to Forget

Can you remember your first day of school? I remember mine well. I was a short redheaded, freckle-faced five-year-old little boy on my way to kindergarten. Jerry Swallows a playmate of mine was also headed on this great new adventure with me.

The Simmons boys who live two houses up the street from us had prepped me for the biggest event coming in my short young life. In great detail they warned me of the horrors that awaited little unsuspecting boys.

They alerted me to watch out for one thing in particular. Located on the outskirts of our town was a *Reform School,* a home for delinquent children as they were called in those days. We passed it each time we drove to the park.

The Simmons boys told me that my elementary school officials would pick out certain little boys, make them line up and then follow a woman out of the room. Those boys would then be driven to *Reform School* and never see their parents again.

We passed through the front doors of the elementary school and Mom dropped me off with the other five year olds. We were sequestered in a big room.

Well, you guessed it. They announced that if your name was called that you were to get in line and follow Miss So and So. I began to cry and did not want to go. I told Jerry to please tell my Mom goodbye for me.

What a mean, dirty trick for older boys to play on an innocent, trusting and unsuspecting little boy. Obviously, there were so many five year olds that school officials were dividing the group into classes and each one was assigned to follow their new teacher to their new classroom. You will never know how wonderful it felt to see my Mom walk through the door and pick me up later in the day.

I was really scared by the whole ordeal. I didn't tell anyone about it but I never forgot it. I've gotten over it but I still have a little chill run down my spine when I enter elementary schools (not really). I moved on, forgave the Simmons boys and Marcus (we called him *Bug*) became one of my closest neighborhood friends.

All of us can relate to experiences about when people have done us wrong. I can remember telling my parents, *that isn't fair*. In a perfect world no one would ever deceive, mistreat or hurt anyone else. But unfortunately we do not live in a perfect world and life certainly is not always fair.

One of the hardest things in life to do is forgive. It seems to come more easily to children. They forgive little conflicts with their siblings and playmates. Within minutes the whole affair is forgotten and they are playing together again.

It is not as simple with adults. The older we get the harder it seems to be to forgive. Forgiveness is an act that does as much, if not more, for the forgiver as the forgiven.

Always Remember

What does forgiving someone who has wronged us do for us?

- It frees us from the control of the inner hurt they've caused us. Many times people who've mistreated us don't lose three seconds sleep over the whole matter. We may carry it for days, months and yes, even years. They completely forget about it, but we relive it over and over again. We are captivated in the prison of our own thoughts.
- Deciding to forgive, even though the person may not have asked for forgiveness, frees us from the prison of our own hurt feelings and helps us move on with life.
- Forgiveness is an essential part of a warm and happy marriage. It was once said that a happy marriage is the union of two good forgivers.
- Forgiveness is essential in the work place if we are to get along with people and be content with our jobs. Forgiveness is essential with our neighbors. I once knew of two ladies who didn't speak to each other for over twenty years because one lady's chickens strayed into the garden of the other. What a waste. Twenty years of friendship sacrificed over some chickens and tomatoes.
- Forgiveness is essential on the highway. I know there are bad drivers out there who cut us off and do inconsiderate things. Forgiving at that moment may keep us from saying or doing something we may regret later.
- The scriptures teach us that if we want peace and God's

forgiveness, then we must forgive others. It is not easy and it sometimes takes us a while to arrive there.

- We are the winners when we forgive.
- We have much to gain when we forgive others and much to lose when we do not.
- So don't stay in the prison of hurt and mistreated feelings.
  - *Forgive early*
  - *Forgive generously*
  - *Forgive completely*
  - *Forgive eternally.*

Forgive and forget - you'll be the WINNER. Remember that old saying, "*To err is human, to forgive is divine.*"

Life isn't fair

That's not fair! I remember thinking and saying that many times as a boy growing up. It would be nice if others always treated us nicely and fairly. But, the truth is that life is not always fair.

I had just celebrated my 20th birthday and found myself learning to become a soldier in the United States Army. Before you could "officially" become a soldier in the Army, you had to successfully complete what was called *basic training*. You learn to march, handle weapons properly, salute officers, and follow orders and a thousand other things.

We had 48 soldiers in what was called a platoon. Our platoon was divided into four squads with 12 soldiers in each. We had one soldier who was the leader of each squad. Our squad leader was lazy and a poor leader. His job was to make sure we were up every morning on time, dressed properly for the day's training activities, our clothes' lockers were organized according to Army regulations and other things.

I didn't want to fail or our squad to get into trouble with our sergeant so I stepped up and helped our squad leader. I actually took over most of his responsibilities and led our squad to successfully complete all the assignments given us, pass all our inspections and graduate from basic training becoming soldiers in the United States Army.

Promotions were given the following week to those who'd shown leadership and excelled during basic training. Promotions meant raising your status in the army with what is called *rank*.

Along with the promotion came an increase in pay.

I remember it like was yesterday! I read the promotion list posted on the company bulletin board. The names were in alphabetical order. Line by line I read each name. MY NAME WAS NOT THERE. Guess What? My squad leader, who'd done nothing, received a promotion. I walked back to the barracks, climbed the steps and sat down on my bunk (bed).

A couple of my friends who were squad members stopped and expressed their disbelief that I had not been promoted and Private _____ had received a promotion.

The more I thought about it the angrier I became. I took my fist and hit the side of my locker and said to myself, *this is not fair*! I did the work and someone who'd done nothing to deserve it was getting the credit, the promotion and more pay.

I heard my sergeant's voice downstairs and decided I'd express my frustration to him. I asked him if we could talk outside. I told him how I'd been the one who'd done all the work and our squad was successful because of my extra efforts. I encouraged him to talk with others in my squad and find out the whole story.

He told me he was sorry and that I was a fine soldier and promotions would come quickly for me. His words didn't mean much to me that night but I learned a valuable lesson, maybe more than one.

I had to make a choice about how this disappointment would affect me. Even at age 20, I believed that if a person worked hard and did the best he could, that good things would come his way. Well... things hadn't gone my way.

I could have let my anger, disappointment, and feelings of not being treated the way I should have been ruin my future view of life. Or, I could learn from the experience and go on with my life.

Always Remember

I chose to learn from my experience. I was determined to be the best soldier I could be. I worked hard and was promoted several times. I was promoted above 17 others in my final promotion and was up for another promotion just before I completed my military service in the Armed Forces of the United States.

What am I saying? Simply, life isn't always fair. You have an idea of how you should be treated and sometimes you will not be treated that way. You can't do anything about not being treated fairly, but you have choices about what you do when you are not treated fairly. It hurts when you feel you're not being treated fairly. You may feel hurt, disappointed and even angry.

Choose not to get even or strike out at the person or situation. Don't let your hurt or angry feelings keep you from the future good things God has in store for you. Ask God to help you. He knows how you feel. Make up your mind that you will work hard and move forward with your life. You will get past this and God will help.

CRITICISM – Who Needs It?

Criticism is part of life. It may come from those who love us most or those who may not even like us. It may arrive like cold water poured on the flames of a great success or like stinging salt in the open wound of a setback.

Have you ever seen a name pop up on your phone and think; Oh no, what is it this time? It almost seems that some people have the *gift* of criticism and feel they should exercise it at every opportunity.

Regardless of whether it is justified or not, receiving criticism is not normally a pleasant experience. How should we respond when we are criticized?

Criticism offered with the right attitude and done in the right way can be a good thing. Criticism, when done in a constructive way to help us, may actually suggest ways to save us problems and create better situations for us.

While serving in my first pastorate in Ahoskie, NC, our church was growing and we desperately needed more room. Our church had a preschool and we were in the process of expanding into a full blown Christian School. We formed the appropriate committees and made plans to construct a new educational building and cafeteria/fellowship hall.

One committee member failed to attend any planning sessions and showed up at the final session shortly before the plans were to be presented to the church.

After he'd looked over the plans, I asked him, "How do you like the plans?"

He responded, "I don't."

My young pastoral fervor got the best of me and I snapped back, "What don't you like about them?"

It upset me that he failed to attend a single planning session and now he wanted to criticize the committee's work. He then showed me a major flaw in the plans. The restrooms were where the offices needed to be and vice versa.

He was absolutely right. We changed the plans and built the new building. I learned a valuable lesson from that experience about the value of criticism.

In Exodus chapter 18, Moses' father-in-law Jethro brings Moses' wife and two sons to join him on his journey to the Promised Land. After a great time of celebration, Jethro observes Moses handling his daily leadership responsibilities. He correctly recognizes that Moses is trying to do too much and will burn out quickly if something doesn't change. He truly has Moses and the children of Israel's welfare at heart.

Jethro first offers the criticism in verse 14. (My paraphrase) Moses' father in law saw all that he was trying to do and asked if he realized what he was doing to these people.

He tells Moses (in verse 17) that what he was trying to do was not good. He then offers Moses a suggestion to help make the situation better.

In verse 21, he encourages Moses to choose good qualified men to handle the small matters and save himself for the major issues that faced the people. Moses' response provides us with a great step-by-step way of handling criticism.

Always Remember

Below are *four simple steps* to remember that may help when people criticize you.

Step 1 - LISTEN to it. Moses heard Jethro out. Have you been introduced to someone you didn't know and became so busy thinking about what you should say and shaking the person's hand that you totally missed the person's name?

A similar thing can happen when we hear criticism. We sometimes throw up barriers because of who is delivering the criticism or simply because we are being criticized.

We need to hold our tongues and *listen* to the details of the criticism before we *speak.* This does two things: It helps us gain a better understanding of what we are dealing with and it provides an opportunity for others to be heard. Even if we choose not to respond in the way others feel we should, they will feel that we've listened to them. Many times just letting folks get it off their chests is all that is needed.

Step 2 - LOOK at it. Moses looked at the details of the plan Jethro had suggested. Once you've heard the criticism, thank the person for bringing it to your attention and tell them that you will certainly give it some thought.

Then seriously examine the criticism/suggestion. Look at the merits of the criticism. Is this a valid criticism? Is there a problem that should be addressed? Are there changes that should be made? Is this person's suggestion the right way to go? You will then know if you should accept or reject the criticism.

Step 3 - LEARN from it. Moses recognized that Jethro was right and implemented his suggestions. If you determine the criticism to be a valid one and the suggestions for change good ones, then don't let your pride hinder you from doing what your gut tells you that you should.

Make the changes. Move in another direction. Implement a new procedure. Stop this or start that. We never reach the place that we cannot learn from others.

Step 4 - LIVE above it. After you've *LISTENED* to it, *LOOKED* at it, *LEARNED* from it and determined the criticism is unjust or not valid, what should you do? Choose to simply to *LIVE* above it.

Sometimes the best response is not to respond at all. Do not spend a great deal of time rehashing the matter. Move on with life. File the criticism in the back of your mental filing cabinet and leave it there. Take the high road and continue doing what you're doing.

***CRITICISM* – Who Needs It**? Criticism is part of life. It will come in times of great success and also great disappointment. It can be valid but it can also be bogus. It can be helpful and also hurtful. However it may come, we should do our best to handle it well.

SPECIAL MEMORIES

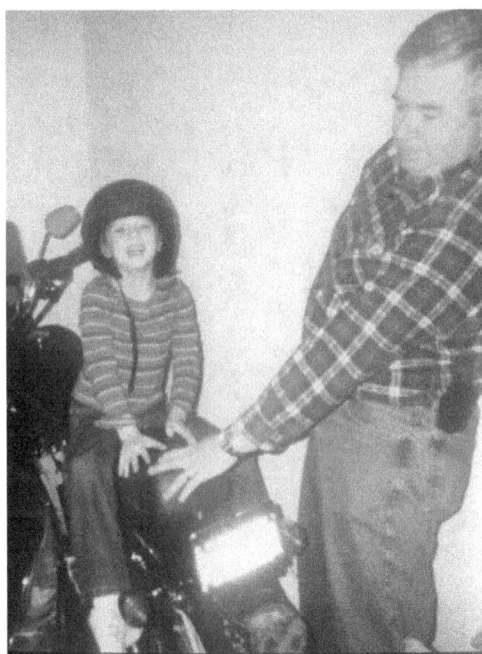

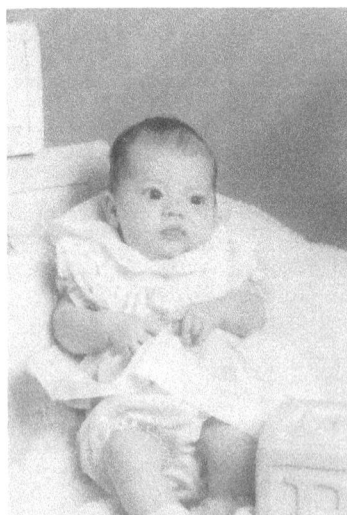

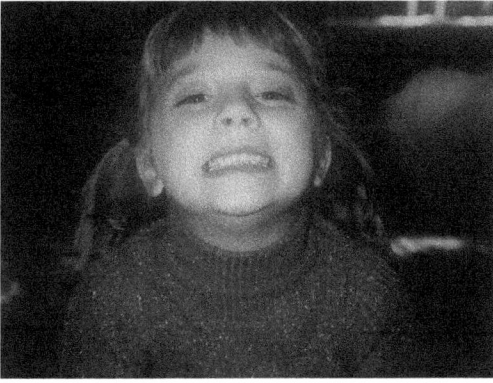

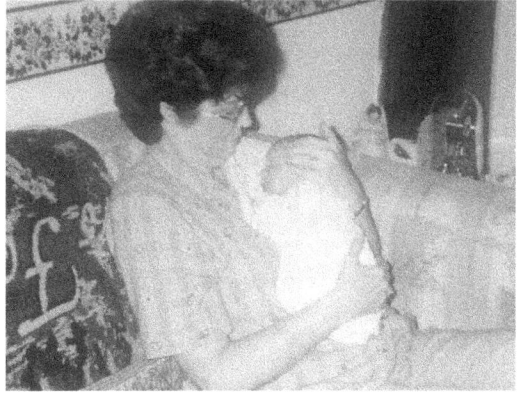

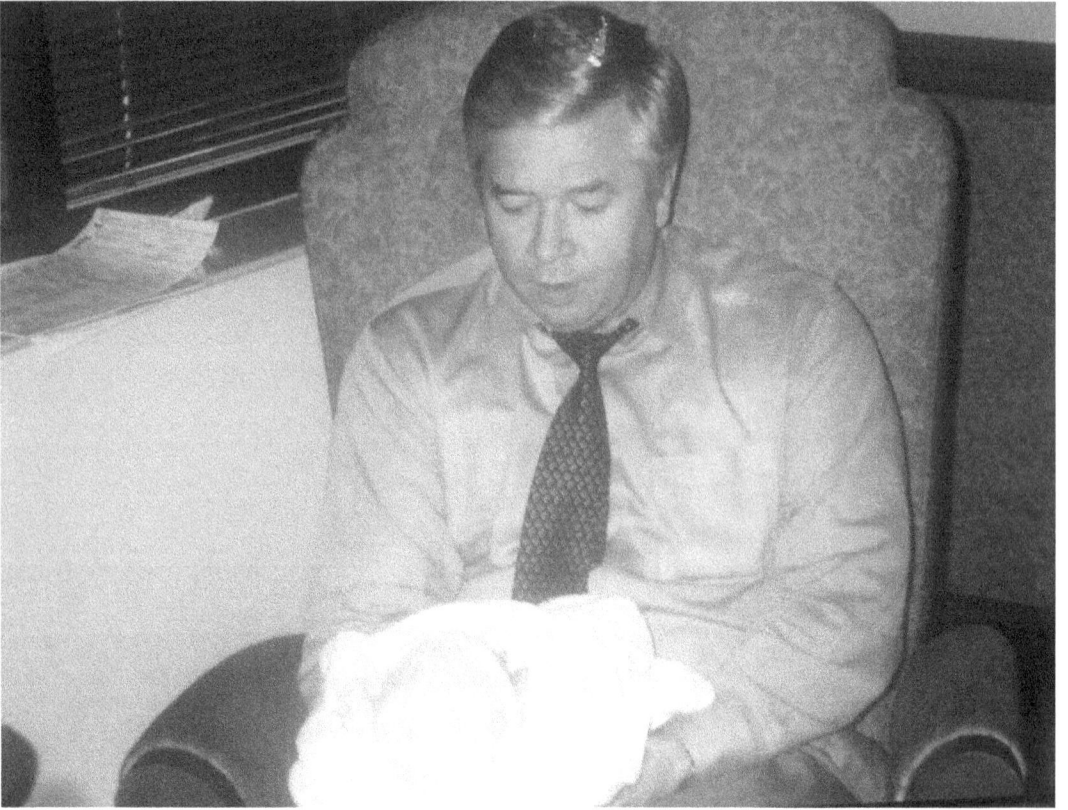

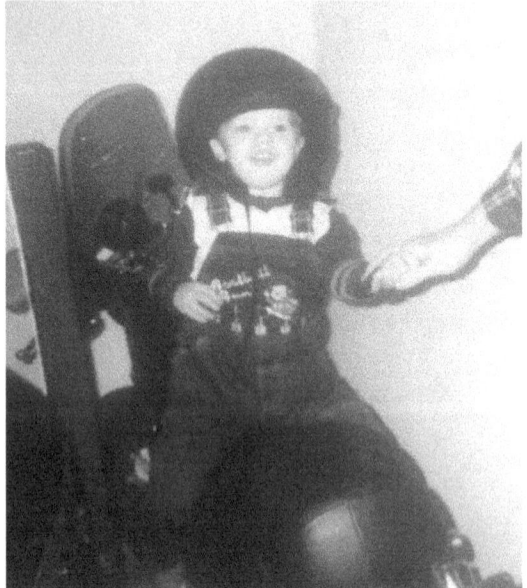

Spiritual Life

Know Christ

Attending church was always a big part of our lives. There was never a question about if we would be going to church. We were there for most every event and for every scheduled service. I was blessed to have parents who were Christians, believed in the Lord and regularly attending church. I was taught about Jesus Christ as a small child. God used the knowledge I'd gained one Sunday morning when I was eleven-years-old.

Reverend Dalton Heath was my pastor and when he preached that Sunday morning, God's Holy Spirit spoke to my heart. I realized that if I died at that moment I was not a Christian and wouldn't go to heaven. I didn't go forward when the invitation was given at the end of his sermon, but something had happened to me.

When Mom, Dad, my brother Rick and I were in the car heading home, I tried to tell my parents what I was feeling. Tears came to my eyes and I had a hard time sharing what I was experiencing. My parents sensed what was happening and called our pastor when we arrived home. They arranged for me to meet the pastor before the Sunday evening worship service at our church.

I will never forget that evening. Brother Heath was waiting for us when we arrived and he, Dad and I made our way downstairs to the basement of the church and into the first classroom on the right. There were neatly lined metal folding chairs in the room and we sat down on the front row. Dad encouraged me to share with the pastor what I'd tried to share with him and Mom.

I explained how the message he'd preached caused me to realize that I was not a Christian and would not go to heaven if I died right now.

He explained how I could know Christ and asked me if I'd like to ask Jesus to come into my heart. We knelt beside those metal folding chairs and I told God I was sorry for my sins and wanted Him to forgive me and come to live inside my heart.

I was changed that night and I've never been the same since.

Always Remember

The most important decision you will ever make is to accept Jesus Christ as your Lord and Savior. This one earthly decision will have eternal consequences.

Don't spend your whole life seeking after things that will leave you empty and unfulfilled. God places within every human being a desire and need to know Him. Know Jesus and you'll find peace, fulfillment and satisfaction for the rest of your life.

How? Look to the Bible, it has the answer.
Jesus said in John 14:6, *I am the way, and the truth, and the life. No one comes to the Father except through me.*

- I like to say it like this; Jesus is the way to the truth that brings eternal life.

- Romans 3:23 reminds us that all of us are sinners.

- Romans 5:8 tells us that even before we were born Christ knew and loved us and took our place and died on the cross of Calvary for our sins.

- Romans 6:23 shows that we deserve to die because of our sins, but God offers us the gift of eternal life through belief in Jesus Christ and what He did for us.
- Romans 10:8-9 tells us how to receive this gift of eternal life.
    - We must believe that Jesus died for our sins.
    - We must believe that he was buried and rose from the dead after three days.
    - We confess with our mouths what we believe in our hearts and ask Jesus to come into our hearts and save us.
- Romans 10:13 gives us the assurance that if we pray and ask the Lord to come into our hearts that He will save us. Not that He might save us or could save us, but HE WILL SAVE US!

The greatest legacy I can leave you is to trust Jesus as your Savior. He has the answer to all of life's important questions.

You Are Special

The Bible tells us in Psalm 139:14 that we are *fearfully* and *wonderfully* made. I want you to know how special you are.

I began working at a restaurant called Burger Chef (similar to McDonald's) when I was 16 years old. I cooked hamburgers and French fries, cleaned rest rooms, burned trash, mopped floors and other tasks and they paid me $1 for each hour I worked.

I worked hard and had risen through the ranks in about a year and at age 17 became the manager of the night shift. I was the boss of eight other employees. I was making my own money, purchasing my own clothes and had even bought my own car. Not bad for a 17-year-old young man, huh?

One day the phone rang and my dad answered the call. My pastor, Reverend Ed Hargis, was on the other end. "Yes, he's here," my father said and handed me the phone.

I was a little nervous. My pastor had never called me before and I wondered what he might want. Our Wednesday evening Bible Study and Prayer Meeting service would begin in a few hours and he asked if I could meet him in his office at about 6:30 p.m., about 30 minutes before the service would begin.

I agreed to meet him having no idea what he might want. I arrived early and we walked to his office together. He asked me to sit down and he sat on the front of his desk facing me.

He said, "Roy, I want to talk with you about something very important. What are you going to do the rest of your life, flip hamburgers? I believe God has something special for you to do."

His words made me angry. I had big plans. I was going to

pursue a career in the restaurant business. I was going to become a millionaire by the time I was 30 years old with the help of the owner of the Burger Chef that I was now working in.

The harder I tried, the more difficult it was to forget what my pastor said to me that evening. I had my own plans and had left God out of them.

I left my manager's job at Burger Chef a few months later to become a freshman at Welch College. I wanted to find out why my pastor thought I was special and what important thing God had for me to do in life.

I prayed and told God I was willing to go anywhere and do anything He wanted me to with my life. That was the best decision that 18-year-old young man ever made. God spoke to me gently through the voice of the Holy Spirit and I came to understand that God wanted me to become one of His preachers. God took my hand that day and He has led me through life on a path He chose just for me.

Always Remember

Psalm 139:14, which we read earlier, tells us that we are *wonderfully made*. That word *wonderfully* literally means *unique* and *special.*

- Understand that God made you unique and you are special.
- Know that you are one of a kind! There is no one like you, never has been or ever will be!
- He made you for a reason and He has a purpose for your life.

- God developed His plan for you before you were born.
- You will never be content or happy until you learn, understand and follow that plan.
- Money and material things will never satisfy the deep longings of your soul. They will not make you happy.
- When you discover God's plan, you will have purpose in life and a reason for getting out of bed every morning.
- Always remember: *YOU ARE SPECIAL* to God and you are *very special to Pawpaw.*

Learn the Scriptures.

Southside Junior High School, my school, required that seventh graders take the Home Economics class and that included boys along with the girls. The school also required girls to take eighth grade Shop class along with the boys.

My Home Economics class was divided into two groups. One group learned how to use a sewing machine, repair clothes and also how to make new clothes. I made a reversible vest with black corduroy on one side and red on the other.

The second group worked in the kitchen, learning the basics of how to prepare basic meals and snacks. The two groups rotated between the kitchen and the sewing area every other day.

The idea behind requiring boys to take the class is so we wouldn't be helpless when it came to a few basic skills that would help us if we had to live on our own later in live.

My group was assigned to the kitchen one day and I was given the assignment of baking oatmeal cookies. I'd never attempted this before and so all of this was totally new to me.

Recipes with directions were written on 3 X 5 inch index cards and kept in a small box on the kitchen counter. I thumbed through the recipes and pulled the card labeled, *Oatmeal Cookies*. The last person who'd used the card had spilled water or some liquid on the card and part of the directions were a little smeared and blurry.

I began to mix the ingredients and came to the point of adding baking soda to the cookie dough. I couldn't quite make out the amount, but it appeared to say ½ cup of baking soda. I added the baking soda along with the other ingredients, stirred, and the dough was ready. I greased a cookie sheet, separated the dough into several small cookies and placed them in the pre-heated oven and set the timer.

I couldn't help but look into the lighted oven and watched the cookies turn from white to golden brown. They looked great and smelled wonderful while cooking. I couldn't wait to taste one.

Ding... the timer sounded and I pulled the cookies from the oven, let them cool a few minutes then placed them on a serving plate. I couldn't resist the temptation and tasted one. Oh, my goodness - it was horrible! My teacher sensed that something was wrong and asked me how the cookies turned out. I told her, "I don't know what happened, but something went wrong."

She tasted one and then asked me what I thought went wrong? I told her I tried to follow the recipe but part of it was blurred and hard to read. I pulled the recipe card from the box and handed it to her.

She asked me to read each of the ingredients and tell her how I'd made the cookies. When I mentioned ½ cup of baking soda, she stopped me. "½ *cup* of baking soda?"

"Yes," I nodded. She had identified the problem. The recipe called for ½ teaspoon of soda instead of ½ cup.

The extra soda caused the cookies to have the horrible taste. She did something I have never forgotten. She told me that it was not my fault. The recipe looked like ½ cup instead of ½ teaspoon and I should not worry about it.

The cooking group always made the food available to the sewing group as well. The teacher placed a sign that said,

SPECIAL COOKIES, PLEASE DON'T TOUCH. She did that so I wouldn't be embarrassed.

I saw one of my friends in the sewing group named Willie English grab a cookie when he thought no one was looking. I kept my eye on Willie. He moved to the back of the room in one corner and took a bite. His eyes seemed to cross and he ran to the trashcan to spit out the bite. Too Funny......

Always Remember

- Remember what we think or believe to be true may not always be correct.

- There is only one accurate measure of what is true, that's the Word of God. What we think or believe to be true doesn't matter if it is contrary to what the Bible says.

- The Bible teaches us in Psalm 12:6, *The words of the Lord are pure words, like silver refined in a furnace on the ground, purified seven times.*

- Learn the Scriptures. The truth of God's Word will set you free. It and only it can show the way to happiness and contentment. John 8:32 tells us, *And you will know the truth and the truth will set you free* (ESV).

- Find a regular time each day to spend reading God's Word and try not to let anything interfere with it.

- Try to read the Bible through once each year. Download a copy of the Bible to your phone or tablet. You'll always have it at your fingertips. There are many easy Bible reading schedules available online you can also download.

- The book of Proverbs is one the most practical guides on how to live, know God, serve Him and how to interact and treat others.

- Read one chapter in Proverbs each day. Start now with whatever day of the month it is and you will read the entire book through in a month. (December 5th read Proverbs 5) Add a couple of extra chapters the last day of the months that have less than 31 days.

Pray

March 1973 found me completing U.S. Army Chaplain School, Chaplain's Assistant training at Fort Hamilton, New York in New York City. I had completed Army Basic Training at Fort Knox, KY in early December 1972 and Advance Individual Training at Fort Dix, NJ in late January 1973.

My daughter Missy was born on February 2, 1973 and I was fortunate enough to be granted leave for a few days. I arrived in Morehead City, NC by bus and made it to Carteret General Hospital one hour after she was born.

Army Chaplain School was much like college. We were recognized as regular soldiers and attended classes Monday through Friday with weekends off. I had completed three semesters at Welch College before being drafted into the Army so the Army Chaplain's environment and classes were comfortable and went well for me.

The Army Chaplain School provided Chaplain's Assistants for the entire United States Army on every post around the world. Each graduating class was highly sought after and ours was no exception.

We learned before graduation that our class was scheduled to deploy on hardship duty to South Korea. It was called *hardship tour* because you had to spend one year in Korea before being allowed to return to the States. Also, your family cannot join you.

I was concerned because I'd just held my first-born child in my arms and I may not see her or her mother for over a year.

Missy wouldn't know her own father and I would miss the first year or so of her young life.

I began praying specifically as soon as I found out where I would probably be deployed. I explained my circumstances to the Lord and that if it could be in His permissive will, I would like to be stationed in a place where my young family could join me.

The weeks passed and the week of graduation arrived. This was it! We would all soon find out where we would serve our country. Word came to our barracks that the list of permanent duty station assignments had been posted on the CQ bulletin board.

I nervously made my way out the door and into the central courtyard moving at a steady pace toward the bulletin board. I trusted the Lord and believed He would do what was best for my family and me.

Soldiers huddled in front of the board. I joined the group and waited my turn. The list was typed in alphabetical order, last names first to the left and their duty assignments to the right.

I stepped to the board and began running my finger down the list. My heart began to sink.

NAME	DUTY ASSIGNMENT
Adams, Bill	South Korea
Brown, David	South Korea
Casper, John	South Korea
Demos, Fred	South Korea

I worked my way line by line and name by name. A, B, C, D, E, F and G. My finger came to rest on Harris, Roy W. I slid it across the page fully expecting to see South Korea. Every soldier so far had been assigned to South Korea.

I could hardly believe my eyes: FORT LEONARD WOOD, MISSOURI. I would be staying in the States and my family would be able to join me in a few weeks. My little girl would know her father and I wouldn't be separated from my family. Tears filled my eyes and I dropped to my knees right then and there and thanked the Lord for His goodness and for granting my request.

I learned later that the Army had done something unusual with our class. The normal procedure was to assign one class to the States and the next to overseas duty stations. They divided our class with half assigned to South Korea and the other half to bases across the continental United States. The line was drawn for overseas stations at my name. From my name on down the list was assigned to the United States; everyone above my name went to Korea. Some might say that was a coincidence; I would say it was the sovereign hand of the omnipotent God. I prayed believing God would answer. He did! He did it in an unusual way and in a way I could not have imagined.

Always Remember

- God talks to us through His word, we talk to Him through our prayers.
- God has what I like to call *His permissive will.* For reasons only known to Him, He allows us, through our prayers, to impact what He will or will not do.
- Our prayers are important, and He listens to what we say because He already knows how we feel and what is best for us.

- Prayer makes a difference.
- Pray often (prayer doesn't have to be with fancy words – sometimes it's simply, *Lord, please help me.)*
- Pray anywhere at any time (You can talk to God riding down the highway or sitting in a restaurant. You don't need to be in church to pray.)
- Praying posture doesn't matter. (You can pray with your eyes open or closed. You can pray standing, sitting, kneeling, lying down. The posture doesn't matter.)
- Pray for specific things.
- Pray believing that God will answer. HE WILL!
- God will always answer your prayers. He may say yes. He may say no. He may say not now, but later. But HE WILL ANSWER!

Understand Your Ego

The Judge focuses the attention of the entire courtroom on the jury box, "Has the jury reached a verdict?"

The chairperson rises from his chair, "Yes, Your Honor we have. We the jury find the defendant…" Many hours of hard work and investigation have led to this moment of anticipation. What will the verdict be?

Have you ever wondered what might be at the heart of many of our problems? The answer might surprise you. You may recall the biblical story of Adam and Eve. In the story, a serpent appealed to Eve's pride. "God is not treating you fairly," the serpent (Satan) told her.

Her pride said to her, "You deserve more and possessing more will make you happy." Pride was at the root of man's first problem.

Another word for pride is *ego*. In 1 Corinthians 3:21-4:7, Paul addresses the root of the problem the Christians had in the city of Corinth located in Asia Minor. The root of their problems was pride and boasting.

We can learn much from Paul's teaching about pride and the human ego. Paul compares the human ego to a physical organ in the body. Normally functioning parts of the human body garner little attention yet contribute greatly to its overall well being and welfare.

When a part of the body becomes injured or dysfunctional, the entire body's attention is drawn to it. The body becomes

—

91

focused on doing whatever is necessary to meet the needs of its injured member. The need to satisfy the injured member takes precedence over everything else.

The human ego is intangible, yet no organ impacts the person more. Paul gives a good description in 1 Corinthians 4:6 of man's ego as inflated with much air pumped into it. It is swollen, inflamed, bigger than it should be, and ready to burst.

This dysfunctional organ called ego dominates the focus of the entire person. The human mind, body, and spirit marshal all of its resources in an effort to appease the needs of the ego. The ego's requirements are ever demanding and never fully achievable.

Timothy Keller, in his book *The Freedom of Self-Forgetfulness* does a great job of describing the condition of the human ego. Notice three characteristics present in the human ego.

First, the human ego is **empty**. It is overinflated with nothing at its core. Soren Kierkegaard's book, *Sickness unto Death* says it well; *it is the normal state of the human heart to try to build its own identity around something besides God*. The human ego searches for self-worth, sense of purpose and feeling special.

Man's ego deceives him with illusions that without God he is competent to run his own life, achieve self-worth and find purpose big enough to give life meaning. King Solomon understood this well. *Vanity of vanities, all is vanity,* he said in Ecclesiastes 1:2. He enjoyed the high position as king of Israel, great possessions, and any pleasure the world had to offer. He understood through personal experience that man's ego is hollow and empty and can never be fully satisfied. Whatever we try to put in God's place can never be enough. It will always be too small.

The *second characteristic* of man's ego is that it is **painful**. It produces pain because there's something seriously wrong with it. Man's ego produces reoccurring, ongoing, daily pain. It draws attention to itself every day.

Man's ego hurts because it's never completely happy. It always makes us think about how we look, what other people are thinking about us and how we are being treated. Our feelings get hurt. Well, it's impossible for feelings to hurt. It is our egos that get hurt because our identity and our sense of self-worth are hurting. It is difficult to make it through a single day without feeling ignored, snubbed, failing to measure up, wondering what others are thinking about us or getting down on ourselves.

There's something wrong with my identity. There is something wrong with my sense of self-worth. All of this causes me pain. There's something wrong with me and that something is my *ego*.

A *third characteristic* of ego is that it is **very busy**. Ego stays incredibly busy trying to fill its emptiness and soothe its pain. Paul gives insight into how ego seeks to remedy this pain and emptiness. He reminds us in First Corinthians 4:6 not to take pride in one person over the other. Man's ego tries to fill the emptiness by *comparing* and *boasting.*

The empty, painful, inward ego-self requires validation. It seeks to secure validation by constantly comparing itself to others. Short-lived temporary relief comes but never lasts long.

C. S. Lewis, in his chapter on pride, in *Mere Christianity* gets it right when he states, *Pride gets no pleasure out of having something, only out of having more of it than the next person.*

We are proud because we have more wealth, a higher position, better looks and more talent when comparing ourselves to others. The empty ego is restocked and the painful need for self-worth, reassurance and value has temporarily been reaffirmed.

This nourished ego quickly becomes hungry again when we come in contact with others who are wealthier, hold higher positions, are better looking or who may be more talented. All pleasure taken in what we had quickly vanishes because in reality we had no pleasure in them at all.

Our egos are extremely busy comparing and measuring others to ourselves hoping to find us better than them. We are desperately trying to bolster our self-esteem in an effort to fill the emptiness and soothe the pain of inadequacy. Pride is the pleasure of having and being more than the next person!

Always Remember

How do we fill the void and eliminate the pain of our inflated egos? By seeking the approval of others? By accepting ourselves? Neither of these works because meeting the standards of others or our own personal standards requires perfection. Therein is the problem.

- We are fallible and perfection is beyond our reach. Paul tells the Corinthians that he is not concerned with what they think of him, neither is he concerned what he thinks of himself. *My conscience is clear, but that does not make me innocent,* he says. The Greek word for *innocent* comes from *the word justify*. This is the same word Paul uses throughout Romans and Galatians. Paul is making the point that justification is beyond his own efforts.

- Our empty overinflated ego has it backwards. It requires us to perform a never-ending search for validation seeking the *verdict* that we are important and valuable.
- The *verdict* is in. God has pronounced us valuable and important. The court of heaven has vindicated us. We have been declared innocent, important, and valuable. The one who judges us is the one who vindicated us.
- Now we perform because of *the verdict* rather than seeking it. Jesus loves and accepts us because we are more valuable to him than the wealth of the whole world.
- Our value and self-worth should not depend on having more money than others, looking as good as somebody else, feeling good enough, etc.
- We should not devalue our self-worth because we are left out, looked over, or looked down upon.
- *The verdict* is in. It's time to embrace *the verdict* and seize our identity, value, importance, and self-worth.
- We are children of a God who created us, knows us, loves us and we are important to him. Let's live our lives accordingly!

Be Grateful

Is your cup of life half empty or half full? Are you a pessimist or an optimist? Life is more enjoyable when we focus on the many good things that have come our way. I'm reminded of the old church hymn written by Johnson Oatman Jr., which was first published in 1897 titled *Count Your Blessings.* The hymn's chorus describes a great way to look at life:

> Count your blessings, name them one by one,
> Count your blessings, see what God hath done!
> Count your blessings, name them one by one,
> And it will surprise you what the Lord hath done.

A great way to fill up the mind's eye cup of life is to identify and express *gratitude* for the many blessings that have come our way.

What is Gratitude?

*G*ratitude is the quality of mindful acknowledgment of all that we have been given and being thankful and showing appreciation for it. That definition is a combination of several but in a nutshell, we should reflect on the good things we've been blessed with, be thankful for them and show appropriate appreciation to those who are responsible for our enjoying them.

Why is Gratitude important?

Gratitude is important because of what it produces in us. We human beings tend to look at life with tunnel vision. We focus on the issues and situations in our lives that are most pressing. Isn't it amazing how one situation or problem can dominate our lives, capture our thoughts and sometimes even harm our relationships? Reflecting on the blessings in our lives brings front and center the wonderful things we possess. Reflecting on those things can stir feelings of thankfulness and gratitude. Reflecting on our blessings and being grateful for them helps lift our spirits and can overshadow those tough problems we may be facing.

Gratitude is also important because of what it does for others. Just as we are impacted by the love and generosity of others, others are impacted by our gratefulness or lack thereof. Recognizing those who may be responsible for many of the good things in life is the first step toward being thankful and expressing gratitude. Although some people do not like public recognition, most people like to know that what they do for others is appreciated. Expressing gratitude to those who contribute to our sense of wellbeing and happiness is always the right thing to do. We all like to know that what we do for others is acknowledged and appreciated. Gratitude on our part is a small price to pay for huge sacrifices many times made on our behalf by others. It will bring a sense of satisfaction and accomplishment on their part and may inspire a desire for them to do even more for others.

What are some things to be grateful for?

One great way to identify things, which should demand our gratitude, is simply to write them down. This can be done in a variety of ways. Many like to keep a journal of each day's events and activities that occur in their lives. One could add a category of *things to be grateful for* in their journal. Another way is to take a minute each morning or each evening to reflect on the good things in one's life. Keeping a *blessings list* on the computer and reviewing and adding to it each day is another way. One can be creative, but the important thing is to identify and reflect on those good things.

What are some of those things? Each person's list will probably be a little different but there are some basic things we should be thankful for and express our gratitude.

- Salvation – those of us whose lives have been gloriously saved and changed through Jesus Christ and have the promise of eternal life have much to be grateful for.

- Health – if we are blessed with good health we should certainly not take that for granted and be grateful.

- Family – if we are blessed with family who love us and make us feel loved and afford us a sense of belonging, we should be grateful.

- Friends – there are some friends who are even closer than family members. God created us with a sense of community and we need that interaction. If we have close friends, we are blessed and should be grateful.

- Basic Needs – if we have food to eat, a roof over our heads and clothing, we are truly blessed. Much of the people in third world countries do not have these basic necessities and we should be grateful.

- Living in America – living in this country with its guaranteed freedoms and opportunities to better ourselves is a great blessing and we should always be grateful.

- And Etc. – why have a category like this? I'm sure you have many things you are grateful for. You can reflect on those and add them to this list.

How full is your cup?

Do you want your life cup to be half empty or half full? That decision is up to each individual. King David, in one of the most beloved and well known Psalms (Psalm 23:5), said this about his cup of life: *Thou preparest a table before me in the presence of mine enemies: thou anointest my head with oil; my cup runneth over.* (KJV) David is celebrating the fact that in spite of being surrounded by difficult circumstances (*presence of his enemies*), that God is supplying his needs and wants (*prepared a table with a feast on it*). Because of this, David is filled with joy (*thou annointest my head with oil. Oil was used at festive entertainments, and was a commonly used to illustrate joy.*) David remembered this each day and the end result was a life cup, which was not only half full but also completely full and overflowing.

Always Remember

Why not consider doing what one verse in the "Count Your Blessings" hymn suggests?

> When upon life's billows you are tempest-tossed,
> When you are discouraged, thinking all is lost,
> Count your many blessings, name them one by one,
> And it will surprise you what the Lord hath done.

- Gratitude is an acknowledgement of all that we have been

given and is the quality of being thankful and showing our appreciation. Focusing on the wonderful abundance in our lives will make the difficult days more bearable, the good days more joyful and engender a greater sense of generosity, cheerfulness and contentment in our lives.

• Showing our gratitude should become one of our good habits. It will: recognize and affirm our appreciation for those who give to us, encourage us to savor each gift that comes our way, open our hearts freeing us from selfishness in hoarding our possessions. Gratitude will help us celebrate God's goodness toward us today instead of being discontent and always waiting on our next accomplishment or receiving a bigger gift tomorrow.

• Fill your life with gratitude for all the good things that the LORD and others have brought into your life. Your life cup will become full and overflowing and your joy and happiness may not only impact you but also the lives of many others. Want to have a better day tomorrow, be grateful today.

Don't Use Curse Words!

We lived at the end of a dead end street in Irondale on East 16th Street in Anderson, Indiana until I was in the middle of the 6th grade. I walked to school and enjoyed playing in the small creek in the woods and the empty field in front of our house.

My first exposure with *cuss (curse) words* came from the mouths of the Simmons boys who lived two doors up from us. I can't remember exactly how old I was but I do remember the event like it was yesterday.

I'd picked up some of the words I'd heard them use and that was not a good thing. My parents didn't use those words nor did any of the people at church. I guess it made me feel older and part of the group when I said those bad words. I was careful not to let one slip around my parents or anyone else for that matter.

A few of us were playing in the field across the street and having a good time as usual. My next-door neighbors, Larry and Cindy, who were younger than me, were also playing with us.

I wanted to impress the older boys so I said something very bad to Cindy using some words I'm too embarrassed to mention in this story. I saw the hurt in her eyes and I wished I hadn't said those words to her. But it was too late! The damage had been done.

Soon I forgot about it and went on playing. Mom arrived home later that afternoon from work and the day seemed pretty normal. There was a knock at the front door and Cindy's mother was standing on the front porch.

My mom joined Minnie on the front porch and a few minutes

later came back into our house and closed the door. She asked, "What in the world did you say to Cindy?"

I felt like the blood was draining from my whole body, starting with my face and working its way down to my feet. I was both scared and embarrassed. The words didn't come easy and I stammered for something that might somehow get me out of the mess I'd gotten myself into.

Needless to say, Mom was not pleased with my response and played the *Dad Card,* "You just wait until your Dad gets home!" Oh my... I knew I was in big trouble. She made me sit on the front porch until Dad arrived home. He told me hello and walked into the house.

My heart felt like it was going to pound right out of my chest. Dad returned a few minutes later. He had a stern look on his face and he ordered me to follow him around the house to the back porch.

He asked me what I'd said to Cindy. I was too embarrassed to repeat it and it was horrible to have him repeat those terrible words back to me. He took his belt off and gave me one of those spankings I'll never forget. He told me that I'd better not say anything like that again to anyone. By the way, I haven't.

Always Remember

There were a number of things I learned from that experience. I noticed some good reasons on the website, *Project Inspired,* that you shouldn't use curse words.

- Cursing can quickly become an unbreakable habit.
- Cursing is dangerous. One word now can quickly become a dirty word in every other sentence. It's just better if you never even start. 1 Corinthians 3:16: *Know ye not that ye are the temple of God, and that the Spirit of God dwelleth in you? (KJV)*

- Cursing can quickly ruin your testimony.
- When you hear cursing at school, the mall, or the park, do you think to yourself, *I bet that man loves Jesus*? What you probably think is that he's probably not a Christian. Is that what you want people to think about you? Ephesians 4:29: *Let no corrupt communication proceed out of your mouth, but that which is good to the use of edifying, that it may minister grace unto the hearers. (KJV)*
- Cursing can cost you friends.
- Do you like being around people who curse? If you see someone with his or her friend who is cursing, don't you identify him with the person who curses? Odds are, your friends won't want to be associated with you if you are constantly cursing. Psalms 10:7: *His mouth is full of cursing and deceit and fraud: under his tongue is mischief and vanity. (KJV)*
- Cursing makes others feel discouraged.
- Cursing at someone is rude and inconsiderate. The Bible says to edify (or uplift) one another, not tear each other down. Romans 15:2 *Let every one of us please [his] neighbor for [his] good to edification. (KJV)*

- People will respect you less if you curse.

- Do you respect someone who can't control his mouth? Cursing will make you seem immature and childish in other people's eyes. It doesn't make you sound "cool". Proverbs 3:7 *Be not wise in thine own eyes: fear the LORD, and depart from evil. (KJV)*

- You never know who's listening when you're cursing, especially if you're in public. There could be young children present. You can never be sure who hears you, so do you really need to say those words? 1 Peter 3:10 *He that will love life, and see good days, let him refrain his tongue from evil, and his lips that they speak no guile. (KJV)*

- God is ALWAYS listening.

- He is disappointed when you curse or use his name in vain.

- Deuteronomy 5:11 *Thou shalt not take the name of the LORD thy God in vain: for the LORD will not hold him guiltless that taketh his name in vain.* Leviticus 19:12 *Ye shall not swear by my name falsely, neither shalt thou profane the name of thy God: I am the LORD*. (KJV)

The decision is up to you. What will you do? Will you curse and disappoint God? Or will you praise and uplift those around you with your words?

"Whether therefore ye eat, or drink, or whatsoever ye do, do all to the glory of God." (1 Corinthians 10:31) (KJV)

Right or Wrong, How Do I Know For Sure?

I challenged you in previous chapters to do your best to always do the right thing and try to never do the wrong thing. Is it possible to always know what you should do? Is there a way to decide what you should or should not do?

Yes there is! The Bible tells us in Psalm 119:105 that the scriptures are *a lamp to our feet and a light to our paths.* God's Word will help you. That verse is saying that God's Word will show us the way we should go and help to keep our feet on the right path.

We also blessed to have God's Holy Spirit living within us to guide us. John 16:13 reminds us that the Holy Spirit will help us know and understand the truth.

I was fascinated in the eighth grade when one of my teachers showed us a homemade radio he'd made using a wooden thread spool with copper wire wrapped around, screwed to a board powered by a flashlight D battery.

We could hear our local AM radio station when he touched the wire to the battery. We lived at 3709 East Lynn Street in Anderson and our garage was in a separate building behind our house. I came home from school that same day and decided I would attempt to make a radio like the one my teacher made.

I saw an old box fan in the garage that no longer worked. That gave me an idea! If my teacher could power his radio with a flashlight battery and reach our local AM radio station WHBU 1240, if I had more power, my radio might be able to pick up one of the Indianapolis stations that were about 35 miles away.

I found a small board about a foot long and six inches wide to build my radio on. I went in the house and found a wooden spool with a small amount of thread on it in Mom's sewing basket. I stripped the thread off the spool and made my way back to the garage. I cut the cord off the old fan, then cut it again leaving about six inches with the plug still attached. I stripped off the insulation exposing the strands of copper wire. I wrapped the copper wire around the wooden spool and attached the spool to the board. I then attached the ends of the left over cord to each end of the copper wire.

The radio was ready (this picture is an idea of what one should look like, mine was similar) – I thought!

I took my *new radio* into the house to try it out. I sat down next to a wall power outlet in our den and plugged the radio in. Poof... Sparks flew from the wall and the radio at the same time and the lights went out in half the house.

Mom and Dad were at the grocery store and would be returning home at any minute. I quickly grabbed my *new radio*, ran back to the garage, climbed up into the rafters and hid the radio in a back corner near the underside of the roof. It's probably still there after all these years.

Dad came into the house and the lights were not working in the den. He checked the fuse box (most homes had fuses and the faulty radio caused the fuse to blow). Dad commented that a storm must have passed through while they were at the grocery store across town and lightning must have caused the fuse to blow. I said, "Well, one thing I know for sure, sparks flew in the room and the lights went out."

To this day, I haven't told him the story about the radio and I'd appreciate it if you didn't tell him either.

There were several problems with the radio and I'll comment on those later.

Not understanding how the radio worked and the right way to build one was my biggest mistake. The result was disastrous.

Not understanding how to make good decisions in life can be even more disastrous. I developed an approach when I was a young man, which has served me well. I want to share that approach with you.

There are **five questions** you can ask that will help you determine, in most situations, what you should or should not do.

1. Does the Bible specifically mention this?
2. Will this build me up or tear me down spiritually?
3. Will this hurt my testimony with other Christians or hinder my ability to witness to the unsaved?
4. Will this physically harm me?
5. Will this help me to be more masculine or feminine or cause me to be immodest?

Always Remember

1. Does the Bible specifically mention this?
The Bible is the final authority on any subject and we should

behave according to what it says to do or not to do. A good place to start is with the Ten Commandments. (King James Version of the Bible)

- First commandment – *You shall have no other gods before me.*
- Second commandment – *You shall not make for yourself a carved image.*
- Third commandment – *You shall not take the name of the Lord your God in vain.*
- Fourth commandment – *Remember the Sabbath day, to keep it holy.*
- Fifth commandment – *Honor your father and your mother.*
- Sixth commandment – *You shall not murder.*
- Seventh commandment – *You shall not commit adultery.*
- Eighth commandment – *You shall not steal.*
- Ninth commandment – *You shall not bear false witness against your neighbor.*
- Tenth commandment – *You shall not covet.*

Here's a cowboy's description of the Ten Commandments from years ago. (Please pardon his spelling and grammar.)

- Just one God.
- Put nothin' before God.
- Watch yer mouth.
- Git yourself to Sunday meeting.
- Honor yer Ma and Pa.
- No killin'.
- No foolin' around with another fellow's gal.
- Don't take what ain't yers.

- To telling tales or gossipin'.
- Don't be hankerin' for yer buddy's stuff.

The Bible says a great deal about what is right and wrong and how we should behave. It addresses idolatry, immorality, character, respect for human life and many other lifestyle issues.

We should first ask the question, *does the Bible mention this area specifically? If so, how does it say I should behave?* The answer to this question may give direction to what our decision or behavior should be. So, *always* ask this question first.

---

2. Will this build me up or tear me down spiritually?
What is the answer? We certainly can't find it within our own experiences. They are too unreliable and depend only on what we have come to know through our five senses.

The scriptures also have the answer in helping determine if what we are thinking about doing might tend to build us up or tear us down spiritually. Philippians 4:8 tells us:

Finally, brethren, whatsoever things are true, whatsoever things are honest, whatsoever things are just, whatsoever things are pure, whatsoever things are lovely, whatsoever things are of good report; if there be any virtue, and if there be any praise, think on these things. (KJV)

Another way of saying this would be: *lastly my friends, keep your mind on things that are true, pure, right, holy, friendly and proper. These things are worthwhile and worthy of praise.*

What are some specific ways in which our minds are impacted by the things we see and experience?

- **Television**
    - ○ What are some TV shows we would be better off not watching because they might tear us down spiritually?
    - ○ What are ways television might help build us up spiritually?
- **Internet**
    - ○ How can it be destructive? Wasted time, wrong relationships could be established, pornographic websites, etc.
    - ○ How can we use the Internet to grow spiritually stronger?
- **Things we read**

    Be careful what you read - magazines, books, etc.
    - ○ Reading the wrong kinds of materials will hurt you spiritually.
    - ○ How can good reading materials build us up spiritually?
- **Movies**

    Be careful what movies you watch.
    - ○ Movies with bad language, nudity, plots that cause those who attend to become desensitized to immorality, adultery and idolatry will make you spiritually weak.
    - ○ How can movies be a positive resource to build us up spiritually?
- **Friends**

- o Be careful about keeping friends who cause you to have wrong thoughts or encourage you to do things that you know are wrong.
- o How can friends be a positive resource to build us up spiritually?

- **Music**

Listening to the wrong kind of music can tear us down spiritually.

What are some other things that might tear us down or build us up spiritually?

If the things mentioned above can impact us negatively and tear us down spiritually, then how can we address these distractions to our good spiritual health?

Here are three steps that can help you answer that second question: *Will what I am considering doing tend to build me up or tear me down spiritually?*

- **Step one – Determine that you want to win the battle and grow spiritually**.

Taking care of the spiritual basics can go a long way in helping you behave in ways that will build you up spiritually instead of tearing you down.

✓ Make up your mind that you are willing to invest your time, talent and resources.

✓ Talk with God every day. – *Prayer*

✓ Let him talk to you. – *Read his word.*

✓   Become involved in a Christian small group.

✓   Regularly attend church services and activities.

•   **Step Two – Remove things that tempt you.**

What are some specific temptations that come to your mind that can weaken your spiritual well being which should be removed from your life?

✓   Relationships with friends, believers or non-believers, who bring us down spiritually should be evaluated and changed if necessary.

✓   Make a conscious decision to avoid certain websites on the Internet.

✓   Get rid of books, magazines, etc. that are suggestive and direct the mind in the wrong direction.

✓   Think about television programs, which are suggestive or may contain content that are contrary to the Bible, and make the choice not to watch them.

✓   What are some other temptations you should remove?

•   **Step 3 – Develop *roadblocks* to head off temptations.**

The best defense is a good offense. Being pro-active will head off temptations before they gain a foothold and cause serious spiritual damage. Name things that you can do to plan ahead that will help you steer away from temptations, which may have caused you trouble in the past.

✓   Make sure nothing of less importance takes priority over going to church and being present for each service.

✓　Set a definite time each day to spend in Bible reading and prayer.

✓　Purchase security software for your computers that may also double as a filter that automatically blocks inappropriate websites.

✓　Cancel magazine subscriptions that borderline on what is appropriate.

It is possible to determine the best behavior for the Christian in every situation. A Biblical standard must be used if we are to be successful. We've asked two questions so far and we'll ask three more that will help us in continuing the development of the Bible based way of determining how we can know right and wrong.

---

3. Will this action hurt my reputation with other Christians or hinder my ability to share the gospel with unsaved?

God uniquely created us and we are also created to enjoy relationships. We are built with a need for relationships with God, ourselves, His creation and other human beings.

We should also remember that we no longer belong to ourselves. Our new life in Christ was purchased at great cost, the suffering and death of Jesus.

Ephesians 2:8-10 tells us that *we are his workmanship, created in Christ Jesus unto good works, which God hath before ordained that we should walk in them.*

- Workmanship
  - The word literally means cut out of the same fabric.
  - It illustrates the craftsman's personal design and work.
  - It exhibits distinct attributes and characteristics that are unique to the craftsman.
- Good works
  - Doing good things and living a good life.
- Before ordained
  - To prepare in advance
- Walk in them
  - A guide to conduct or govern one's life

The verse reminds us that we are the creation of a master craftsman, Christ Himself. We are created in God's image or *cut out of the same fabric*. We are created for one important purpose, to behave in a way that reflects in a good way on our creator. This was part of the blue print of our design even before we were created.

1 Corinthians 8:13 says: *Therefore, if food makes my brother stumble, I will never again eat meat, lest I make my brother stumble.* (NKJV) The controversy at the church in Corinth was over eating certain meats. Meat could be bought in the market place at a good price because it was left over from sacrifices to idol deities. There was great discussion over whether Christian people should purchase and eat the meat.

Paul emphasized the meat itself had no power. He makes

the point that there was a difference of opinion on the matter between the Christians at Corinth. Paul said there was nothing wrong with eating the meat, but some who had worshiped idols and sacrificed to them before they became Christians had a real struggle with the idea of purchasing and eating those former instruments of worship.

- Christians sometimes disagree about what we should or should not do.
- Some things seem wrong to some people and others think they are OK.
- The outside world has an idea of how Christians should live - what they should do and what they should refrain from.

We must have a way to measure right and wrong, good and best. Most Christians have similar Bible based convictions of right and wrong, but they tend to disagree in the matter of standards. Standards and convictions are terms which tend to be used interchangeably, but they also seem to be relative, meaning different things to different people.

What are convictions and standards? A conviction is something that never changes and I am willing to die for it. A standard is something which could change, but I choose to live by it.

Here are some things that would be classified as convictions that never change.

- The Bible is the inspired Word of God and contains no errors.

- There is only one God.
- Jesus Christ is God's Son.
- Jesus died on the cross for the sins of all mankind.
- Christ is the only way to God.
- Every person is responsible to God for his or her own actions and will one day stand before Him to account for their choices on earth.

Paul came up with a great principle that we can apply. We should not purposefully do anything that we know is offensive to a fellow Christian. He emphasizes that we have a right to our own opinion on issues that are not a matter of violating biblical convictions. He recognized, even in his day, that there were cultural differences between the Jewish Christians, including himself, and the Gentile converts. He felt the differences between the cultures could be accommodated.

He wanted both groups to understand that there were differences of opinion and both were right. Each group had the right to make behavioral choices. He used the meat offered to idols as a great way to highlight the problem and offer a solution.

His solution was for both groups to respect the opinion of the other. For those who were offended by eating meat offered to idols he said, *If you know meat has been offered to an idol and it offends you, don't eat it*. For those who had no problem with the meat he said, *If it doesn't offend you, eat the meat.* He felt it was important for both groups to respect the other's feelings on the matter.

He instructs the non-idol meat eaters when sitting down at a fellow Christian's home, not to ask where the meat came from, thus respecting the host's feelings. He instructs the host to respect the feelings of his guest by not serving meat that he knows might violate the guest's conscience if he or she knew.

Truly, our behavior will impact both saint and sinner alike. It is very important to set our standards of behavior with other Christians and unsaved people in mind.

---

4. *Will this action harm me physically?*

Take a minute to read 1 Corinthians 1:15-20. The church at Corinth had many internal problems. One major problem was sexual immorality. Paul uses this occasion to remind the Christians at Corinth of some important things regarding their bodies.

He takes the approach of asking questions that should have easy answers. Here are a few of those questions.

- Don't you know that your bodies are members of Christ?
- What does *being in Christ* mean? When we become Christians, we are rescued from spiritual death. We are born again into God's family. Just as we have our parents' blood flowing through our veins when we are born that forever connects and identifies us with them, we are now connected to God the Father by Christ's blood. In a figurative sense, we take on God's last name if He had one. His royal stamp forever identifies us with Him.
- Don't you know that sexual immorality creates a sensual

bond with another person that is in direct conflict with the bond we have with Christ?

Genesis 2:21-24 reveals God's perfect plan of morality: *one man, one woman for one lifetime*. Something mysterious and special happens between a man and woman who are married that cannot be fully understood or explained. The physical consummation in marriage forever changes the identity of the husband and wife. They no longer have totally separate identities, but rather share a combined identity with two personalities.

When God's perfect plan of morality is violated or tainted by immorality, the people involved are forever impacted in negative ways.

Paul is saying there is a serious problem with those who sin using their bodies with others and claim to be in harmony with the *one Spirit* relationship with Christ. It makes no sense to think a Christian can live in immorality.

Paul asks another question:

- Don't you know that when a person commits immorality, even though it is done on the outside of the body, it is a sin against the whole body?

How does immorality affect the person committing this physical sin in a negative way? Sexual sins seem to be in a category all their own. The lasting personal impact is almost immeasurable. First of all, the person committing this type of sin feels guilty. A concept of what is sexually and morally right is built deep within every human being. Sinning against one's body begins with the guilt of knowing wrong behavior has occurred.

A second negative consequence is never being able to remove the act completely from the mind. Even though God forgives and forgets, human beings have a more difficult time. The human mind is a giant recorder of thoughts and actions. Once an act has been committed and recorded, it is difficult to completely erase it from the mind. Even though one has asked and received forgiveness, he or she still has a hard time removing the mental scars.

One final consequence is the devastating impact on family, friends, church members and the unsaved world. Families have been torn apart because of one act of sexual indiscretion. Friendships have been destroyed and churches divided because of immoral behavior. One who commits immorality hurts not only himself/herself, but also the harm goes far beyond the individual.

Paul asks another question:

•   Don't you know that your body is a temple (dwelling place) of the Holy Spirit of God and He lives within you?

Let's try something for fun. Go online and do a search for two of the most prominent dwelling places of God in Jewish history, the tabernacle of Moses and temple of Solomon. The tabernacle was mobile and the temple was permanent. The tabernacle was made of cloth and skins and the temple of rock and mortar.

One key thing they had in common was that both were symbolic of the earthly dwelling place of God. Paul carries over this symbolism as a way to illustrate the importance of the human body and the inseparable spiritual relationship it has with God.

God no longer resides in a manmade central place of worship. He now lives in every Christian through the person of His Holy Spirit. The implications are enormous. The Holy Spirit is present in the Christian no matter where he or she goes or whatever they do. This should remind us not to place our bodies in locations and do things we wouldn't want God to see and know about.

Paul asks another question:

• Don't you know that you do not belong to yourselves? Do you think God has the right to own our bodies? We were created with a free will. God made the supreme payment for our sins with the death of His Son. We accepted a *paid in full* receipt for our sin debt. In exchange, we gladly handed over the deed to our earthly physical dwelling places (our bodies).

Let's bring this down to everyday life. Paul reminds us in 1 Corinthians chapter 6 to glorify God in our bodies. What does this mean and how can we do it? What are some specific things we should and should not do as Christians? We discussed one obvious immorality earlier. We should avoid immoral behavior and live holy lives before the Lord. Improper sexual behavior must be avoided at all cost.

What are some other things that impact our bodies that should be addressed and how we can take care of our bodies? Here are a few possibilities:

• *Gluttony*
• *Junk Food*
• *Yearly Physical at the Doctor's Office*

- *Regular Exercise*
- *Prolonged Sun Exposure*

5. *Will the action I'm considering enhance my masculinity or femininity or compromise my modesty in any way?*

There is a principle called magnetic force. When a magnet is placed near certain objects, those objects are naturally drawn to the magnet. When a magnet passes near other objects, those objects ignore the magnetic force.

We have human magnetism as well. How we appear to others will impact them and us in positive and negative ways.

There is an incident of the first meeting of a future husband and wife that illustrates the importance of modesty, masculinity and femininity.

Take a few minutes and read Genesis 24:62-66. What quality stands out with Rebecca's actions? She shows her femininity by the way she was dressed and her modesty in the way she conducted herself in her first meeting with her future husband.

What does modest, masculine and feminine mean? Here are some possible definitions:

- **Modest –** Bashful, reserved, self-conscious, humble, discreet and unpretending.
- **Masculine –** Brave, macho, manly, red blooded, powerful, gallant and muscular.
- **Feminine –** Delicate, gentile, girlish, ladylike, soft, tender and unmanly.

Projecting an appropriate image as a Christian is crucial in being what we need to be as Christians. Our society tries to blur the distinctions between the sexes. Can you see this and is it true? Why? What are some ways in which this is happening?

There are moral implications of diminishing the distinctions between the sexes. Always remember that all sinful actions begin in the mind. Wrong attitudes come before wrong actions.

Staying sexually pure begins in the mind with the correct attitude. Looking at the way you think about your modesty, masculinity or femininity can be a great first step towards protecting yourself from straying into impure thoughts that might lead to impure actions.

Do you think it is possible for one person to cause impure thoughts in another person? If not why not and if so, how?

Remember modesty is being reserved, self-conscious, humble and discreet. How are attitudes translated into actions? Proverbs 25:6 tells us: *Do not exalt yourself in the presence of the king, and do not stand in the place of the great.* (NKJV) This verse shows us the virtue of modest behavior. The wise writer instructs us to act in appropriate ways that do not draw inappropriate attention. How can we attract the improper attention?

- o The way we dress
- o The way we talk
- o The material things we possess

Titus 2:1-6 tells us *But as for you, speak the things which are proper for sound doctrine: that the older men be sober, reverent, temperate, sound in faith, in love, in patience; the older women likewise, that they be reverent in behavior, not slanderers, not given to much wine, teachers of good things, that they admonish the young women to love their husbands, to love their children, to be discreet, chaste, homemakers, good, obedient to their own husbands, that the word of God may not be blasphemed.*

Likewise, exhort the young men to be sober-minded, in all things showing yourself to be a pattern of good works; in doctrine showing integrity, reverence, incorruptibility, sound speech that cannot be condemned, that one who is an opponent may be ashamed, having nothing evil to say of you.

Notice the appropriate actions of the following mentioned in the passage:

- Older men are not to go overboard but live worthy of respect and exercise self-control.
- Older women are to live holy lives, stay away from alcoholic beverages, and show the younger women by word and example how to live modest and caring lives.
- Younger women are to control themselves, live pure lives and take good care of their homes.
- Younger men are to control themselves and do the right thing.

Remember the five behavior principles which help us determine right and wrong and how we should behave in any situation:

1. *Do the scriptures mention this specifically?*
2. *Will this tend to build me up or tear me down spiritually?*
3. *Will this hurt my testimony with other Christians or hinder my ability to witness to the unsaved?*
4. *Will this harm my body?*
5. *Will this enhance my masculinity/femininity or compromise my modesty in any way?*

Right or Wrong – can you know for sure? ABSOLUTELY! I have great confidence in you and I know that with God's help you will know and do the right thing.

Family Life

Don't Live Together Outside Marriage

Later today I will counsel with my second couple this week in preparation for their upcoming wedding. This reminded me of something I've wanted to do for some time, address the question of why marriage is important. I do not claim to have all the answers but I do speak as one who has experienced the wonderful joy of being married for a total of 38 years.

Our modern American culture has seemingly declared war on the oldest institution in the history of the world, marriage. It has sought to diminish the importance of marriage and relegate it to the dark closet of the old fashioned and declared it to be out of step with the times. Why address this? According to Michael McManus' book *Marriage Savers,* the problem has become epidemic. The number of couples living together outside of marriage has increased by 1200% since 1960.

There are problems when marriage is not valued. I've sat in living rooms of couples who were living together while unmarried and heard them say things like: *we don't need a piece of paper to commit to one another for life, we aren't hurting anyone,* or *it's our business and nobody else's.* A culture that embraces this approach on face value without proof simply has not looked at the facts.

Eight out of ten couples that live together before marriage will break up either before they marry or at some point after they marry. Couples who live together before marriage and eventually do get married are *50% more likely to divorce* than those who do not. *Only 12%* of couples that begin their relationship with cohabitation end up with a marriage that will last for ten years.

What about the statement; *it's nobody else's business and we aren't hurting anyone anyway*? Well, I would beg to disagree! It is our business because cohabitation does hurt others.

Again, the statistics bear this out. Children living in homes where couples are unmarried are *five times* more likely to grow up in poverty than those with married parents. These children are *twenty-two times* more likely to be *arrested* and end up incarcerated. These children are *three times* more likely to be expelled from school and *three times* more likely to end up in teenage pregnancies. These children are *ten times* more likely to be sexually abused by a stepparent than those growing up in homes with their birth parents.

This lifestyle does impact the lives of others and it should be a concern to all of us. Divorce, child abuse, teenage pregnancy, high school drop outs and career criminals are a few problems that have already arisen from a culture that has sought to diminish the value and importance of marriage.

God has a planned relationship for society. Reading and following directions usually will provide a better outcome than simply taking all the pieces and trying to make them work with no plan. God supplies the directions on how a society can survive and thrive. He began his instructions with the first institution he created and blessed. God created Adam and helped him understand that he was alone and needed someone to complete and enhance his life (Genesis 2).

God reached next to Adam's heart and took a rib and created Eve. He brought her to Adam and blessed their newly established relationship. Have you ever thought about why so many people want church weddings? I believe a key reason is that they want God's blessing on their new life together.

God creates men and women to complement each other. They need each other and supply those things, which are necessary to find happiness and contentment. God established this paradigm for mankind. A man and a woman are united under God in the institution of marriage. Man is to leave his father and mother and establish a new family of his own. He is to *cleave* (like glue) to his wife. The man and woman *become one flesh*.

Sexual relationships outside marriage are strictly prohibited and sexual behavior contrary to God's standard is considered to be a sin on the same level with other major sins according to 1 Timothy 1:9-10 (murderers, *whoremongers, homosexuals,* kidnappers, and liars) and 1 Corinthians 6:9 (*fornicators,* idolaters, *adulterers,* effeminate, abusers of themselves with mankind will not inherit the kingdom of God.) Departure from God's standard brings spiritual death. It is serious business to deviate from God's plan and produces serious consequences.

Always Remember

Marriage has great benefits.

According to *The Case for Marriage,* by Dr. Richard Niolon, married couples do better financially. They share furniture, food, insurance benefits, cars, etc. When one person becomes ill, loses his or her job, or needs emotional support, the spouse is there to help.

Married men are more successful in work as well, getting promoted more often and receiving higher performance appraisals. They also miss work or arrive late less. Married women earn 4% more than their single peers.

Married people live longer. Based on life expectancies, *nine of ten* married men and women who are alive at age 48 will be alive at 65, while *only six of ten* single men and *eight of ten* single women make it to 65. Married men may have better immune systems as well, either from support of a loving wife or her nagging to monitor blood pressure, cholesterol, weight, etc... and may be at less risk to catch colds (Cohen et al.)

Married men are half as likely to commit suicide as single men (Smith, Mercy, and Conn). Married people report lower levels of depression and distress, and 40% say they are very happy with their lives, compared to about 25% in single people. Married people were half as likely to say they were unhappy with their lives.

Who needs marriage?

The American society needs it. According to the Word of God, cohabitation (couples living together outside marriage) is sin. It is the sin called *fornication*. Not a pleasant word and one we do not use or hear very often in our churches, much less our culture.

But it is sin and is devastating to all it touches. Its tentacles reach far beyond the couples involved. It impacts our homes, our children, our churches, our schools our law enforcement personnel, our prisons and more.

Marriage is a benefit to society and brings longer, healthier and happier lives to those who participate in it. Let us all do more to exalt the virtues of marriage, admonish the violations and volatility of simply living together. A man shall leave his father and his mother and shall *cleave* (loyal and unwaveringly) unto his wife: and they shall be *one flesh* (Genesis 2:24).

Career

Keep Your Word

Missy had just turned four-years-old and Aaron was about to turn one. We were living in Goen Hall, the main men's dormitory at Free Will Baptist Bible College (Welch College) in Nashville, TN.

I was the Resident Director, in charge of five men's dormitories, about to finish my senior year, earning my Bachelor of Arts degree.

A married student near my own age had a set of Expositors Commentaries for sale for $80. I was planning to become a pastor after graduation and was continually trying to add to my library. A pastor's library contains his tools for trade and is crucial in being well read and staying prepared to do a good job for his congregation.

I agreed to purchase the commentaries although our income was very limited. We had an unexpected expense and it became very difficult to find enough money to purchase the commentaries.

I asked the student if I could talk with him about the commentaries and he agreed. I began to explain about our situation and the unexpected expense. I asked him if it might be possible to not purchase the commentaries or maybe buy them later when we had more money?

He interrupted me before I could complete my final sentence. He emphatically let me know, in no uncertain terms, that I had told him that I would buy those commentaries and this was not his problem. He expected me to buy the commentaries and pay for them on time.

He seemed uncaring and showed no sympathy for our financial situation and what we were facing. He was right. I told him earlier that I wanted the commentaries in good faith. But our circumstances had changed and now I could not afford them.

I had two choices; purchase the commentaries as I had promised or simply walk away from the whole situation. I will have to admit this was quite a struggle for me. We were nearing the end of the semester and school year and more expenses would be coming in a few days. I still had to make the final payment of my school bill for the semester.

The decision was made before I walked away from him that day. He was not willing to work with me and had no compassion or sympathy for our situation, but I made a promise, given my word, and I had tried to do the right thing most of my adult life. When I say that I will do something, I have every intention of doing it.

So I told him I would have the money by a certain date and when that day came, he received his money and I took the commentaries to my office. No pleasantries were exchanged and I must say that I was not very comfortable at that moment in that situation.

But I kept my word and did what I said I would do. I also realized this young man would probably have trouble later in life. He had no sympathy or compassion for others, and his self-centered attitude made life all about him. I am not a prophet, but he did have serious trouble later in life.

Always Remember

There were a number of lessons I learned from that experience.

- Make the decision to be a person of your word!
- Be careful when you say, *I will do this* or *I will not do that*.
- When you say you will do something, do it!
- When you say you will be somewhere, be there!
- There will be times and situations where it may be difficult or even impossible to keep your word. Face this sooner rather than later. Communicate with the appropriate person or institution and explain your situation, and why you are not able to do what you said that you would do. Offer an alternative solution and make arrangements to keep your commitment (word).
- Your reputation and credibility will be impacted in a huge way with how you give your word and then keep it.

I paid the man the money I promised and God took care of all of our needs. I finished my senior year at Free Will Baptist Bible College and paid my final school bill payment.

I kept my word and have tried to keep my word ever since that day. I do my best to carry out things I promised, be where I say I will be, and do what I say I will do. I'm not perfect by any means, but I want to be known as a man of integrity who strived to do the right thing and keep his word.

SO KEEP YOUR WORD! YOUR WORD SHOULD BE YOUR BOND! If you hope to be a person who is known be honest and a person of integrity, begin by ALWAYS KEEPING YOUR WORD.

Strive for Excellence

Ninth grade at South Side Junior High was a great year for me. I was considered an upper classman and would move on to Madison Heights High School the next year.

I played on three sports teams, earning letters in cross-country, basketball and track.

I enjoyed Biology class and the cool things we dissected. One requirement for Biology was to write a full-blown term paper. I had written a minor version in eighth grade on the Battle of Shiloh for Mr. Melson, but this would be much different.

I actually enjoyed doing the research in the library. I prepared 3 x 5 index cards with information for the paper, along with sources, page numbers, etc. It came time to write the paper and the writing went well.

I was careful to make sure my facts were accurate, but I made one big mistake. I failed to document my sources correctly. I was not careful about placing the footnotes in the correct order.

I didn't think it would matter, but I was wrong! The teacher gave us a reading assignment at the beginning of class and announced that he was about to grade my term paper. I was nervous but felt good about what I'd written.

The teacher sat at his desk in the back of the room and I saw him get up and move to some of the resource materials on the back wall of the classroom. I wasn't sure what he was doing, but I was sure that it couldn't be good.

He called me to his desk after a few minutes and pointed to one of the footnotes. A volume of the World Book Encyclopedia was also open. "Your footnote says your information came from this page and I cannot find it." He pointed to a second footnote and another page in the encyclopedia and repeated the same statement.

I told him that I'd gotten confused and had not been as careful as I should have with the footnotes. He said, "Mr. Harris, you did a great job in researching the subject and writing the paper, but your lack of attention to one of the most important details is a major problem. Return to your seat."

I was so disappointed. I was proud of the paper but knew that I'd not been as thorough and careful as I should have been in citing my sources.

Our term papers were returned a couple of days later and I dreaded seeing my grade. A big red D was at the top of the page. I don't remember the exact words he wrote but they were something like, *You would have received a much higher grade if you'd paid more attention to your footnotes.*

I went on to finish the course with a C knowing I could have had at least a B. I graduated from high school, earned a Bachelor of Arts degree in college, a Master of Ministry degree with honors and a Doctor of Philosophy degree from Trinity Theological Seminary with honors.

Always Remember

I learned some valuable lessons from that experience.

- Details are important. Don't take shortcuts that might come back to hurt you.
- Always do your best and don't settle for just getting by or just good enough.
- Striving for excellence will help you succeed. You'll accomplish more, be recognized more often by others for your work, and be given more and more responsibility as you move through your chosen career.
- Do your best even when no one else is around or watching you.
- Remember that God instructs to always do our best. *Whether you eat or drink, or whatever you do, do all to the glory of God* (ESV). I Corinthians 10:31
- Always give it your best effort *–STRIVE FOR EXCELLENCE.*

Finances

10, 10, 80 – Handle Your Money Well

The year was 1980 and I was 27 years old. I'd accepted the pastorate of the Ahoskie Free Will Baptist Church in Ahoskie, NC after serving as Resident Director, then Dean of Men at Free Will Baptist Bible College (now Welch College) for the past four years.

We would move to Ahoskie at the end of the month and were making preparations to leave Nashville. I visited the Free Will Baptist National Offices to talk with the Board of Retirement Director Herman Hersey about setting up a retirement account.

I had fond memories of Herman playing the piano and Bill Gardner singing at our church camp in Indiana when I was teenager. (I also remember beating Herman at Ping-Pong.)

Herman and I sat down and he talked with me about my financial future. I remember the advice he gave me that has been very valuable. Herman said, "Roy, every $10 you save now will multiple to $40 when you reach retirement age."

I opened a retirement account that day and deposited money in it and other savings accounts for almost 40 years. Herman was absolutely right. I'm so glad I listened to his advice. The money I deposited has more than quadrupled and I now have over $....... No, I'm not going to tell you how much, but it is truly amazing how a little saved at a time has become a lot with the interest it's earned.

Always Remember

- Your greatest asset is the money you will earn.
- The greatest source of future income will partly depend on how well you handle that money.

I came across a simple financial equation when I was in my twenties that has worked well for me and I believe it can for you also.

We'll call it the *10-10-80 Plan.*

- Tithe 10% (I will say more about tithing in another chapter.)
- Save 10%. Saving part of your income is so important!
  - o It will enable you to take care of unexpected expenses like car repairs, replacing a washer or dryer when they quit working, repairing a burst water pipe, paying the deductible for a medical expenses and etc.
  - o It will also make it possible to purchase a home because you've saved enough money to make the down payment and pay the closing costs.
  - o But more important, when you reach retirement age you'll be able to enjoy a comfortable retirement receiving monthly income from the money you saved.
  - o Don't make the mistake of thinking you will live comfortably from the money received through Government Social Security. Social Security was created to help with retirement and not take the place of good planning and saving for retirement.

Here is an example of how the money you save can

multiply. Begin saving by age 22 and this is the money you'll have to live on when you reach retirement age:

- At $20 per week (about $80 per month) you'd have $331,553 by age 67.
- At $40 per week (about $160 per month) you'd have $663,105 by age 67.
- At $50 per week (about $200 per month) you'd have $828,882 by age 67
- At $100 per week ($400 per month) you'd have $1,657,765 by age 67.

- Learn to live on the remaining 80%.
  - Learn to live within your means. Live on the money you earn and receive.
  - Be careful not to develop a *buy now, pay later* approach to life.
  - Don't borrow from *your future* to live in *the present* by paying high interest on credit cards.
  - Buying things on credit and monthly payments will quickly eat up your spendable income.
  - Never charge more on a credit card than you can pay off at the end of the month.
  - Never pay just the minimum credit card payment. You'll end up paying twice as much as you charged.

Here is an example of what it will cost and how long it will take you to pay off credit card charges only making the minimum payment.

- If you charge $5,000 on your credit card,
- With an APR interest rate of 15.99%.
- If you only make the minimum payment of $110,
- It will cost you over $12,000 to pay off the original $5,000.
- It will take you an estimated 25 years to pay off the original $5000 you charged.

The Apostle Paul told Timothy in 1 Timothy 6:10 that *the love of money is the root of all kinds of evil (ASV)*. Money is necessary and we need it to obtain food, shelter, clothing and the basic things of life.

- It is not wrong to possess money, but when money possesses you then it becomes wrong.
- Take good care of your money and later in life your money will help take care of you.
- Buy what you need, but need what you buy.
- Remember, life is more than food, shelter and clothing.
- Jesus told His disciples in Luke 12:22-24, *do not worry about your life, what you will eat, about your body, or what you will wear. Life is more than food and the body more than clothes. Look at the ravens: They do not sow or reap; they have no storehouse or barn, yet God feeds them. You are much more valuable than the birds!*
- Give the God who gave you 100% the first 10% of your income. That will be the best investment you will ever make.

You Should Tithe

Why should you give God the first 10% of your income? Let me tell you why I did and still do and why you should too.

I Tithe Because My Parents Did.

The Sunday morning began like most. We finished breakfast. Mom was putting the final touches on her lady-like appearance. Dad, my brother Rick and I were in the den watching The Gospel Jubilee providing us with a enjoyable mix of Southern Gospel Music from The Blackwood Brothers, The Goodmans and numerous other singers.

Dad, leaning forward in his recliner, picked up his checkbook from an end table. He filled out a check paid to the order of: First Free Will Baptist Church, Anderson, Indiana. He signed, folded and placed the check in his shirt pocket. He would later slip it from his pocket and drop in an offering plate as an act of worship during the Sunday morning Worship Service.

I was in my mid-teens but I remember this Sunday morning routine well. This was not the first time I witnessed this act. This was Dad's *practice* every Sunday morning for as long as I can remember.

Why do I tithe? My parents taught me to tithe. They believed in and practiced tithing when I was a boy, and 45 years later they still do. They talked about tithing in front my brother and me. They told us why they tithed. They described ways in which God had blessed our family because they tithed. They even scared us a little by mentioning others who they knew didn't tithe and how those people paid the tithe in medical bills, car repairs and other unforeseen personal expenses.

They made such a strong case for tithing that my brother and I didn't know we couldn't tithe as boys growing up in Albert Harris' household.

I Tithe because I know tithing is a good investment.

I remember reading Malachi chapter three in my early days as a student at Welch College. I'd read that passage before, but now I was in college away from my tithing parents and had begun choosing my own path in life.

God spoke to my heart that day in a direct and meaningful way. I understood Him to say through His Word, "*Roy, why not test me. If you'll be faithful in tithing, I'll take care of all your needs and give you more than you can imagine for the rest of your life. I'll take what you give me, multiply it and then give back much more to you than you've given me.*" (Malachi 3:10-12)

I made a commitment to God that day and believed in His commitment to me. I've remained faithful to my tithing commitment for over forty years and I can say without hesitation that God not only kept His commitment to me, but He has given me far more than I could have imagined when I was that eighteen-year-old young man.

I've made numerous investments in a variety of venues, which have produced good results. I can truly say the greatest investment that has yielded the best return is the heavenly investment of the tithe and offering.

I Tithe because the Bible tells me to.

God's holy Word is clear on the matter of tithing. There are numerous sources that give detailed descriptions and scriptural evidence for God's requirement of the tithe from every Christian believer.

I think Malachi 3:8-9 is sufficient here to reinforce God's demand for the tithe. God instructs us in verse eight that men rob God when they do not give tithes and offerings. It's a dangerous thing to steal from God. How dangerous? I wouldn't want to offend the one who holds my entire financial future in His hands. Verse nine says those who rob God pay a heavy price. Instead of receiving God's favor and blessings, they are cursed and will receive God's disfavor.

I Tithe because it is God's plan for supporting the local church.

God instructs us in Malachi 3:10 to bring the tithes into the storehouse. Obviously, the local church is God's modern day storehouse and is the depository for the currency of the tithe. I give my tithe to my local church and then give my offerings to wherever God directs.

I do not have to pray about the minimum I should give or where I should give it! God has clearly defined that in his Word. A minimum of 10% of my income is to be given to my local church. From there, the sky is the limit on how much and where to give offerings.

Always Remember

Parents, please remember your children are watching. They will *do as you do* rather than *do as you say.* Parents want children to enjoy the best life they possibly can afford. The most beneficial financial package and legacy parents can leave their children are examples of Jesus Christ in every way and that includes *returning the tithe* and *giving an offering* above the tithe.

You may wonder why I used the word *return* the tithe instead of *give*? The simple truth is the tithe *already belongs* to God. We actually *begin giving,* when the tithe has been returned to God. The *offering* follows the *tithe* and becomes an offering once the tithe threshold has been met and is returned to God.

Want a hot tip on a good investment? Learn to live on 90% of the 100% God gives you. Put God to the test. Return the 10% that *belongs* to Him and watch how He will multiply it and give back to you above and beyond what you thought or imagined.

The scriptures teach us that *God loves a cheerful giver.* Want to make God happy? Return the tithe to Him, as recognition that you understand the 100% you receive is His gift to you.

Give an offering above the tithe as God directs you to show your appreciation for all He sends your way. You might be surprised what a wonderful satisfying feeling you experience each time you *return the tithe* and *give and offering*.

Why do I Tithe? A better question might be: *Why wouldn't I?* What about you?

MORE THINGS TO ALWAYS REMEMBER

Final Thoughts From Pawpaw

1. *Live one day at a time*. Yesterday is gone and tomorrow will never come because when tomorrow arrives it will be today.

2. *Worry is a waste of time*. Don't spend your time worrying. If it is something you have no control over, worrying will only make your life miserable. Statistics prove that 85% of what we worry about will never happen and will not be worth the time and anxiety we spend.

3. *People will disappoint you.* People are human and not perfect. They will do and say things that may hurt and disappoint you. Learn to accept this and move on. Try to remember the good things about the person and try to forgive and forget the hurt.

4. *Don't hold on to hurt and angry feelings.* I've learned in life that if you hold onto hurt and anger, you will suffer much more than the person you are angry and hurt with. They probably won't lose any sleep over it and they probably could care less. On the other hand, if you harbor the matter in your heart you will become focused on something which cannot help you. To the contrary, it can hurt you deeply. Anger and hurt feelings can cripple you emotionally and cause you to become obsessed with the whole situation. Let it go! Ask God to help you forgive and forget. You may have to do this several times. Just Do It! You'll be so glad you did. That will be your only hope of moving on to future happiness.

5. *Find ways to serve others.* There are two kinds of people in the world; givers and takers. Be a giver. Find ways to help and

encourage others. Serving brings a great deal of satisfaction and will make you happier than being served by others. Look for ways to serve. When my children were at home and fairly young, I used to do something to help keep them from an argument and teach them a lesson. It we had only one candy bar, piece of cake or etc. I would let Missy or Aaron cut the piece in half and the other one had the choice of the first piece.

6. *Be people centered and not self-centered.* Try not to *one-up* with your experiences and stories. Don't always have one more experience bigger than theirs or a story that will top theirs. Focus on others when you are interacting in conversation. Don't let it always be about you. Ask about things that you think might be important to them like their family, job, church, ministry and health.

7. *Grow up and find your place in the world.* Your goal should be to find your place in life. You can't live with your parents the rest of your life. You should be seeking ways to become independent and making a life for yourself.

8. *Be thankful.* You have a roof over your head, clothing, plenty of food to eat. You were born in country where you have the freedom of life, liberty and to pursue happiness. You can live where you want, work where you want, travel any place you want to go without fear or permission. You have so much to be thankful for. *Count your blessings, name them one by one, count you blessings, see what God has done.*

9. *Learn to enjoy life.* You can choose to embrace life or dread it. Look forward to each day as an opportunity. Get up in the morning with the knowledge that God has given you a new day

and has things for you to do that day. Learn to enjoy each day with all its blessings, opportunities and hopes.

10.   *Seek God first in your life.* Jesus tells us in Matthew 6:33 that if we seek God and His Kingdom first, all of our needs will be met.

11.   *Seek God's will and plan for your life.* The Bible tells us in Proverbs 3:5-6 to *trust in the Lord with all your heart, and do not lean on your own understanding. In all your ways acknowledge him, and he will make straight your paths.*

12.   *Be careful whom you date and marry.* The Bible makes it clear that Christians should not date and marry those who are not Christians. 2 Corinthians 6:14 says, *Do not be unequally yoked with unbelievers. For what partnership has righteousness with lawlessness? Or what fellowship has light with darkness?* Don't fool yourself by thinking you can or will change the person after you are married. That might happen but it's been my experience in observing others that most of the time is doesn't. Understand that you'll have to live a lifetime with this important decision. Seek God's guidance and pray for Him to guide you to the right person. Fifty years alone is better the five minutes of marital abuse and unhappiness.

13.   *Get a good education.* A college degree will open many doors for you. The society minimum is a Bachelor's Degree, but a Master's Degree will put you much further up the line.

14.   *Get a job and become a good worker.* Work was instituted in the Garden of Eden when God gave Adam the job of taking care of the Garden in Genesis 2:15. Matthew Henry's Commentary says, *Even in paradise itself man had to work.*

None of us were sent into the world to be idle. He that made our souls and bodies, has given us something to work with; and he that gave us this earth for our habitation, has made us something to work upon. The Bible also gives instructions in 2 Thessalonians 3:10 that we are to work to supply our basic needs. The Bible reminds us that a person who will not take care of his/her family is worse than an infidel. (1 Timothy 5:8)

15.   *Be on time!* Being on time does a number of things:

    a. Demonstrates you are diligent and dependable

    b. Shows you honor your commitments and you can be trusted

    c. Shows you have respect for other people and that you care as much about their time as your own

    d. Sets a good example for your children and others who look up to you

    e. Builds self-confidence and success

    f. You'll respect yourself!

    I would suggest not only being on time, but *try to always be early*. I would rather be *30 minutes early* than *five minutes late*. You will arrive early by leaving early. By planning to leave early, you allow yourself time for the unexpected problems that could have caused you to be late. Believe me, people will have a higher opinion of you if you arrive early rather than being late.

16.   *The way you dress matters.* You only get one chance at a good first impression. The way you look and dress matter.

    a. If you dress sloppy and look unkempt, people will perceive you as a person who is undisciplined and lazy.

b. Dress modestly. If you wear clothing that draws improper attention to yourself, don't be surprised if others have a lower opinion of you than you'd like. Dress in ways that project confidence, modesty and femininity or masculinity. Dress and act like a lady and people will treat you like a lady. Dress and act like a gentleman and people will treat you like a gentleman.

c. It is *better to be a little overdressed* than underdressed. I try to find out what the appropriate dress for the occasion will be. If I'm not sure, I try to err on the side of caution. People will respect you more if you are slightly overdressed than if you show up dressed down.

d. The way you dress will *impact the way you feel about yourself.* If you dress for success, you are more likely to be successful. If you dress less than your best, you're more likely to have a lower opinion of yourself that could translate into lowering your expectations of yourself.

17.   *Stay away from tattoos*. I remember when I was a young boy seeing a preacher in one of our church revivals wearing a long sleeved white shirt in the middle of the summer. We had no air conditioning in the church and it was hot. Most preachers in those days didn't wear coats and ties in the summertime.

The preacher made a statement I've never forgotten.

He told us that we might be wondering why he was wearing a long sleeve white shirt? He told us the story of how he'd covered both arms with tattoos when he was in the U.S. Navy. He wore the long sleeves to cover some of the tattoos he felt were embarrassing for others to see.

I felt like he was speaking directly to me when he said, "You boys listen to me. Don't make the mistake I did. You may think it's popular because others are doing it, but remember, you'll have to live with it the rest of your lives."

I see young ladies in minimum wage jobs with tattoos on their faces or necks knowing that they'll have a difficult time ever getting a high profile, high paying job. Tattoos may seem cool because you see others doing it. Don't make that mistake. Twenty years from now, you'll be sorry, I promise you.

18.   *READ!* Be a reader. The world is at your fingertips. Access to the Internet makes reading a 24-hour opportunity.

   a. Reading keeps you fresh and from becoming stale.
   b. Reading will keep you up to date on the world around you.
   c. Reading will help you talk more intelligently with others.
   d. Reading will expand your vocabulary. New words make their way into the English language every year.
   e. Reading will improve your focus and concentration.
   f. Reading will improve your imagination.
   g. Reading will improve your memory.

h. Read for the sheer enjoyment of it.

i. Don't every stop reading. You'll never be too old to learn.

19.   *Be careful with credit cards.* Credit and debit cards are a necessity in the modern world. Be careful with your credit card. Don't borrow from tomorrow to indulge yourself with material things today. Don't sacrifice your future spending power on the impulse spending of today. Do not charge more than you can pay off at the end of the month, as credit card interest is the highest interest you will pay. Sometimes you will pay up to 20%.

Credit cards can be a great tool and you can earn points by using them that can be turned into cash or redeemed for other things. Wisely using a credit card has financial benefit. Misuse will cost you a small fortune.

www.ingramcontent.com/pod-product-compliance
Lightning Source LLC
LaVergne TN
LVHW081323060426
835511LV00011B/1829